SOUTH INDIAN CUSTOMS

SOUTH INDIAN CUSTOMS

P. V. JAGADISA AYYAR

GYAN

Published by

GYAN

Gyan Publishing House
5, Ansari Road
Daryaganj, New Delhi-110002
Phone: 011-47034999, 9811692060
E-mail: books@gyanbooks.com

Distribution Network
gyanbooks.com
India, USA, Canada, UK, Australia, France

ISBN : 978-81-212-4049-9 (PB)
First Published, 1925

2nd Impression 2020

Printed at: Gyan Press, Delhi.

South Indian Customs
Author: P. V. Jagadisa Ayyar

FOREWORD

I HAVE great pleasure in introducing to the public this book on *South Indian Customs* by Mr. P. V. Jagadisa Iyer. He is already well known to fame as the author of various works explaining many aspects of South Indian life, custom and tradition. His reconstructions of the past and his interpretations of the present have not a mere academic value but a practical value. They are a stimulus to our taking an intelligent interest in our customs and institutions. Such a stimulus is the best means of preserving the spirit of such customs and institutions and thereby making the society self-conscious, united, purposive, prosperous and progressive.

Social customs and institutions have a new dignity and value to those who regard them as the expressions of the communal will and the crystallizations of the communal experience. They are the self-expressions of the racial genius and are designed to secure the greatest good of the greatest number. Sister Nivedita has well called custom 'the jewel casket of humanity.' The spirit of the custom is the jewel. Should we not try to preserve both the jewel and the casket?

The collection of the folk-lore and the folk-songs of India is an urgent national task. The universal steam-roller of modern civilization is fast standardizing and macadamizing life into a mere motorcar highway. All the old pleasant byepaths and lanes and shady nooks and blossomed bowers are being fast civilized out of existence. Enthusiastic and discerning workers like ensue and that he should be cured of certain ailments. He has absolute confidence in his doctor and in the efficacy of his drugs. So he takes the medicine and implicitly obeys the instructions given to him. The same may be said to be the case with the originators of the Hindu customs and the people that follow those customs. Even as the patient had confidence in his doctor and his drugs so had the followers of a custom confidence in the sages of their land and in their wise instructions.

It has been the experience of not a few that a problem that defied hours of labour and exertion was understood if handed to a cleverer individual even before he began to explain the question. The reason of this is not far to seek. The man of stronger intellect was able to influence the weaker by his mental strength and the understanding of the question asked. The latter begins to understand the problem himself without any verbal explanation. The same principle may be applied to the emotional aspect also. A bad man by the mere proximity of a good man is uplifted a bit from his own lower level.

If what is stated above is grasped and understood, then the influence exerted by the observances of this or that custom will also be clearly understood. An individual follows a custom or observes a rite or a ceremony with the belief that it would do him good. The other people who are present on the occasion encourage him in that belief and strengthen the same with the force of their individual belief. Thus his belief grows stronger and stronger day after day after each observance of such custom, rite or ceremony. Eventually the particular custom, rite or ceremony becomes his one ideal and he believes firmly and very strongly that it is worth living for and dying for. This belief in the long run uplifts him to very high levels.

There is a very interesting myth to illustrate the truth of the above statement. There was an individual who was regarded as a very pious and holy man but in fact he had no strong belief in anything. A simple-minded ryot approached him and humbly begged him to initiate him in the simplest possible form of worshipping and showing his love and devotion to God. He had brought a mango fruit as a present to his would-be preceptor. The holy man having eaten the fruit carved out of the stone in it an image of *Siva liṅgam* and handed it to the ryot. Though very crude in the formation the ryot took it and in the simplicity of his heart asked him whether the deity would eat and if so what it should be fed upon! To be rid of the importunity of the ryot, he said that the deity would eat half a dozen measures of rice cooked and served properly and sent him away!

Returning to his humble dwelling with the priceless Siva image of mango fruit stone, the poor ryot did not know what to do to get six measures of rice every day! TAKE CARE OF TO-DAY AND TO-MORROW WILL TAKE CARE OF ITSELF' thought he and began to exert himself to procure the six measures of rice for immediate use. 'WHERE THERE IS A WILL, THERE IS A WAY' and strange to say that the ryot got his six measures of rice without much difficulty!

Full of love and devotion to the deity of his heart, he carefully cooked the rice, unaccustomed though he was to the process. He placed the food prepared on a big plantain leaf in front of the image given to him by his *Guru* or preceptor. He coaxed it to eat the food even as a mother would coax a dearly loved child. Do what he would, the food remained there and the deity would not eat! The thought that he was perhaps imposed upon by his *Guru*, never for a moment occurred to the simple-minded fellow. It was of course how it should be. The deity was obstinate and would not understand what was good for it even as a stubborn child though hungry. What does the mother do to make a stubborn child eat? She punishes it of course. So his beloved deity should be punished for its own good!

With heart rent with grief for what he had to do he took a whip in his hand and dealt blow after blow upon the image, when lo! the food disappeared in a trice! The ryot was filled with delight and ecstasy! Not a day passed but he procured somehow or other the requisite quantity of rice which when cooked and placed before the deity, disappeared in space in a miraculous manner!

The *Guru* hearing of this from his pupil one day would not believe his ears. He went to the ryot's house to witness the marvel in person. The food was prepared and placed before the deity, but it did not disappear as usual. The ryot was angry and took up the whip when lo! the *Guru* was blinded by a dazzling light for a moment and when he was able to see, he found himself alone in the hut of his disciple! The deity had disappeared with its beloved devotee, having of course eaten all the food placed before!

The spirit of intense devotion pervading through the entire myth narrated above is typical of the pervading every one of the observances of the customs, rites and ceremonies of the Hindus.

A young woman is told that she should sacrifice the wealth of her luxuriant hair, her pride and beauty no doubt, to please the all-powerful deity on the sacred hill at Tirupati or some other similar holy place. She neither hesitates nor murmurs. Her hair is clipped close and laid as an offering to the deity with great joy, reverence and love.

A custom requires that he or she should starve on particular occasions. The requirement is complied with most scrupulously and whole-heartedly. Any amount of bodily discomfort and suffering would be put up with to satisfy the requirements imposed upon the observers of the customs, rites and ceremonies and that too gladly, patiently and calmly.

When questioned as to whether the non-observers of the customs and those that are of other religions are beyond the pale of the divine grace, a true Hindu simply shrugs his shoulders and says in reply 'GOD AND CHILDREN ARE WON BY MAKING MUCH OF THEM':

Besides what has been set forth above, specific customs have specific purposes to serve. The Indian custom of observing distance pollution, etc., has hygienic and sanitary considerations in view. In general the so-called pious and religious people are generally most scrupulously clean and hence contact with people of uncleanly habits is nauseating to them. Any smell, good or bad, affects one in a greater or lesser degree according to the distance greater or lesser between him and the object from which the smell emanates. In the same way people living on unwholesome food such as rotten fish, flesh, garlic, etc., as well as people of filthy and uncleanly habits throw out of their bodies coarse and unhealthy magnetism. This affects the religious people of pure habits and diet injuriously. So they keep themselves at a safe distance which has been fixed by the sages of old after sufficient experience and experiment. So distance pollution has nothing but the purpose pointed out above behind it.

In the manner shown above, every one of the Hindu customs can be shown to be based on not only a religious standpoint but also the standpoint of hygienic, morality, medicine and general utility.

P. V. JAGADĪSA AYYAR.

CONTENTS

SOUTH INDIAN CUSTOMS

CASTING OFF THE EVIL-EYE

Of the innumerable customs prevalent among the Hindus, the one under our notice is perhaps the most common. The eye is the most important of the centres in the human system where the soul-force is concentrated and is radiated from on all sides. In fact the eye is said to be a magnet of intense potency to direct the invisible currents in nature, electrical and magnetic, radiating from the sun—the store-house generator of all such forces. The sun is the light-giver and the eye the light-receiver. If this fact is fully grasped the rationale of the custom will become intelligible.

In this connection it is interesting to notice that children are supposed to be highly susceptible to the influence of the evil-eye and the reason for this is not far to seek. That the most attractive period of human life and in fact of the life of all animals is that of childhood, is a fact well-known to all. There is also a proverb to illustrate this statement that 'Even a donkey is attractive during its sucking period.'

No one can help admiring a beautiful kitten at play and the frolicsome pups of a home pet-dog. Even the ugly buffalo when young is beautiful to look at. Such being the case, it is no wonder that children draw the attention of a number of people, which directs various invisible currents towards them, carrying in their wake undesirable creatures in the invisible worlds, liberating injurious influences. As the counteracting force generated by the children is reduced to a minimum by their undeveloped stage of growth, they are liable to suffer if developed grown-up people do not come to their rescue. The concourse of attention of a number of people towards a particular object may be said to surround that object with invisible matter akin to poisonous matter. A counter-current would carry away all undesirable accumulations clearing the locality as it were. This is effected by various ceremonies and *mantrams* (incantations) casting off the evil effects of the evil-eye. Further, certain substances serve as traps to catch undesirable pests, for example, a fly-paper to catch flies, a piece of paper coated over with sugar to attract the ants, and so forth. Similarly a mixture of turmeric and slaked lime by the nature of its vibrations thrown into the invisible world, full of undesirable super-physical pests capable of affecting human beings very injuriously by the cumulative liberations of magnetism thrown out by a large crowd of these invisible pests if they happen to surround an object or person, draws them towards it to be easily cast out.

It will be a common sight everywhere in India that fields having fertile crops and trees and plants in gardens laden with luxurious fruits, are decorated with fantastic and ugly looking scare-crows and figures made of straw and clay. Even houses that are being newly built have such figures or a melon going by the name *pūshanikōy* (pumpkin) suspended in front. On marriage occasions balls of food mixed with lime and turmeric (in place of blood of slaughtered animals perhaps ?) are waved round the bridal pair and cast on all directions east, south, north and west. A ring pass-not is formed by pouring round them water or waving or carrying round them lighted camphor or a burning light. All these serve the purpose of gathering the pests at particular objects such as the scare-crow or the melon, to free from their troubles the crops, and men engaged in building operation, to grow or perform their work unhindered. These pests, when once gathered at particular places, would remain there if a safe resting place is afforded them. Physical objects serving as clogs hindering the play of forces cause more or less lasting and permanent eddies, on which these pests are left assembled.

In the absence of physical objects, eddies are formed by natural invisible forces playing from pole to pole, on which these find temporary resting places to be thrown out and reinstated time and again by the appearing and disappearing eddies.

So every custom of the Hindu has a rational basis behind which lapse of time and gross materialism of this material age has thrown into the background to be brought to the forefront once again when the materialistic crust is removed and washed away !

PUTTING ON OF CASTE-MARKS

Of the innumerable Hindu customs the wearing of different caste-marks by different sects of people, is one of the most prominent. The Vaishnavaites or the followers of Vishnu—one of the Hindu Trinity—are sub-divided into two sects, one sect wearing a caste-mark slightly different from the other. One sect goes by the name of Vadakalais, meaning thereby those belonging to the northern division and the other by the name of the Tenkalais, i.e., those that belong to the southern division. Those belonging to the first sect wear the U-shaped caste-marks and those that belong to the second sect the Y-shaped mark.

The Madhvas, another sect among the Hindus, who are also Vaishnavaites (at least, the majority of them), the worshippers of Vishnu, wear the caste-marks using a kind of earth called *Gōpi Chandana.*

The Saivaites, the worshippers of Siva, use ashes, sandal and vermilion as caste-marks; vermilion is generally used by women of all sects.

The marks are worn on different portions of the body, the spot between the eye-brows being considered the most important. The next important place is considered to be the centre of the chest. The crown of the head is also considered a proper position to put the caste-mark on as well as the region of the navel. Besides these portions, there are also other important places of the body selected for putting the caste-marks on. In all, there are twelve regions of the body where the caste-marks are worn.

The customs are intensely interesting when we study

their rationale. From a hygienic standpoint, we may say that the caste-marks absorb and help the evaporation of water from the body. The marks are generally worn after a bath. Most people who are religiously inclined avoid hot or tepid water and bathe only in cold water at all seasons of the year. We know that certain portions of the body indicate the temperature of the body more clearly than the other portions. We generally place the hand on the chest or up the temples to see whether the body is hot or cold. So we may safely presume that the centres selected as suitable for placing the caste-marks on, are spots favourable for the absorption of water from the system by the materials used for forming the caste-marks. Thus from a hygienic standpoint we may say that the wearing of the caste-marks after a bath secures immunity for the wearer from the danger of catching cold.

Another important purpose served, by different caste-marks, worn by the people, is that of identification. In former times, different teachers arose establishing different religions in various parts of the country. The teachers and their immediate disciples wanted to know at a glance which among the assembled multitude were their followers. Hence various devices were resorted to. Some had secret signs and pass-words to find out those they wanted. The mode of dress was another of such devices as well as the caste-marks.

We may take the case of the different nations of the world. At a mere glance at the mode of dress, we can say the nationality to which one belongs. Similarly, by the caste-mark one wears, we may say the sect to which he belongs.

The Hindus believe that the sun and the various planets of the solar system are the centres in a mighty consciousness having a huge body formed of fine tenuous matter. In this huge body, there are a number of small bodies like the cells of our body. Each of these bodies, when sufficiently magnified, will be exactly like the mighty body referred to above. Further each of these smaller bodies has a central sun with the other planets. Just as the rotation of a big wheel makes the smaller wheels also attached to it rotate at rates proportionate to the size they bear to the big wheel, the movement of the planets, sets agoing these smaller planetary systems in our bodies also. Each of the centres vitalizes one or the other of the physical organs in man. For example, we all know that the source of all light is the sun. Without the sun we cannot have light and without the light we will not be able to see the objects. The organ of sight is the eye. So, people worship the sun to preserve the eye-sight from harm. To illustrate this, there is also a proverb which means, 'THERE IS NO USE OF PRAYING TO THE SUN AFTER THE EYESIGHT IS LOST.' Similarly each and every one of the organs is said to be influenced by this or that planet. So by putting caste-marks, people indirectly set themselves *en rapport* with the various planets and draw vitality from them. In this way people secure immunity from harm to the various organs of the body.

MUTUAL SALUTATION

Of the several Hindu customs, the one of prostrating before images of God, elders and great personages is unique and worthy of consideration and notice. Although the custom of mutual salutation is not one exclusively peculiar to the Hindus but is shared by the other nations as well in common, yet the mode of performing it, is peculiar with the Hindus as the same is peculiar with the other nations. The basic principle underlying the custom is the same with regard to ' mutual salutation,' among all nations. It is to denote the recognition of soul and soul-force. It is believed that the force generated by the soul in its field of electricity and magnetism is stored in three important centres of the body and made to radiate from there to different parts, just as the nerves in the body are made to radiate from the ganglionic knots.

When people raise their hands joined together either to the chest or to the forehead when saluting, the action is intended to mean ' I recognize and revere the soul—the spark from God manifesting through these centres.' When they simply repeat certain formal expressions of salute, they mean that they go to the root and recognize the soul itself directly, and revere it.

The Hindu custom of prostrating before elders admits of diverse meanings. In the first instance, when one prostrates before his elders, he means that he recognizes the wisdom of experience in him due to his age; when the custom is taken and viewed from an ordinary standpoint it expresses humility. It tantamounts to saying ' I am like dust of your feet.'

When viewed from a higher spiritual standpoint, the custom is intended to ask for a blessing from the mouth of the elder. *Vox populi, vox Dei*, the voice of the people is the voice of God. So when a number of people bless or curse an individual, it amounts to a blessing or curse emanating from God, and it is certain to bear fruits, at least the blessing or curse of a really good man, though this may not appeal to the modern youths who have begun to neglect this custom *in toto.*

Moreover, a personage saluted is under an obligation to bless the individual saluting him. The very act of blessing emanating from the mind agitates matter and this force or rather the wave of matter surcharged with the force of love and good-will should pass over the whole body of the person blessed. So a posture most favourable for receiving the current or wave of blessing is the prostrating posture.

A field is viewed by different persons with different feelings. An agriculturist would view it from his own standpoint of raising corn on it. An engineer would consider whether a railway line thrown across it would not serve a particular purpose of facilitating transport of goods, and people. A mineralogist or geologist would think of the possibility of striking a gold mine or a diamond vein underneath. Though the field looked at is the same, the feeling inspired by it in different individuals is not the same but different. Similarly among men, the love borne by a mother towards her child is quite different from the love she feels for her husband. The feeling inspired by one in a mother is quite different from that in his teacher. The mother views him perhaps as a portion of her body and takes a pride in him, whereas the teacher takes stock of him from a mental standpoint and with admiration. Hence the blessings emanating from people would not be of the same feeling.

A mother would perhaps bless him with long life and happiness, with a strong and healthy body. The teacher may bless him with further enlightenment, and a relative with general well-being and prosperity. From this perhaps has arisen the custom of raising the joined hands to the belly, to the chest, to the brow, above the head and so on, according to the individuals saluted and the nature of blessings solicited. It is ordained in the Hindu *Sāstras* that a mother should be saluted with the joined hands placed at the pit of the stomach.

The *Institutes of Manu* on this subject makes mention of the following :—

'When a superior sits on a couch or bench, let not an inferior sit on it with him ; and, if an inferior be sitting on a couch, let him rise to salute a superior.

The vital spirits of a young man mount upwards *to depart from him* when an elder approaches ; but by rising and salutation he recovers them.

A youth who habitually greets and constantly reveres the aged, obtains an increase of four things ; life, knowledge, fame, strength.

After the word of salutation, a Brāhman must address an elder saying, "I am such an one," pronouncing his own name.

If any persons, *through ignorance of the Sanskrit language*, understand not the import of his name, to them should a learned man say, "It is I," and in that manner he should address *all classes* of women.

In the salutation, he should pronounce, after his own name, the vocative particle *bhōh* ; for the particle *bhōh* is held by the wise to have the same property with names *fully expressed.*

A Brāhman should thus be saluted in return : "May'st thou live long, excellent man ! " and at the end of his name, the vowel and preceding consonant should be lengthened, *with an acute accent*, to three syllabic moments *or short vowels*.

That Brāhman, who knows not the form of returning a salutation, must not be saluted by a man of learning : as a Sūdra, even so is he.

Let a learned man ask a priest, when he meets him, if his devotion prospers ; a warrior, if he is unhurt ; a merchant, if his wealth is secure ; and one of the servile class, if he enjoys good health ; using respectively the words, *kusalam*, *anāmayam*, *kshēmam*, and *ārōgyam*.

He, who has just performed a solemn sacrifice and ablution, must not be addressed by his name, even though he be a younger man ; but he, who knows the law, should accost him with the vocative particle, or with *bhavat*, *the pronoun of respect*.

To the wife of another, and to any woman not related by blood, he must say, " *bhavati* and amiable sister."

To his uncle's, paternal and maternal, to his wife's father, to performers of the sacrifice, and to spiritual teachers, he must say, " I am such an one "—rising up to salute them, even though younger than himself.

The sister of his mother, the wife of his maternal uncle, his own wife's mother, and the sister of his father, must be saluted like the wife of his *father or* preceptor : they are equal to his *father's or* his preceptor's wife.

The wife of his brother, if she be of the same class, must be saluted every day ; but his paternal and maternal kinswomen need only be greeted on his return from a journey.

With the sister of his father and of his mother, and with his own elder sister, let him demean himself as with his mother, though his mother be more venerable than they.

Fellow citizens are equal for ten years ; dancers and singers for five ; learned theologians, for less than three ;

but persons related by blood for a short time : *that is, a greater difference of age destroys their equality.*

The student must consider a Brāhman, though but ten years old, and a Kshatriya, though aged a hundred years, as father and son ; as between those two, the young Brāhman *is to be respected as* the father.

Wealth, kindred, age, moral conduct, and fifthly, divine knowledge entitle men to respect ; but that which is last mentioned in order is the most respectable.

Whatever man of the three *highest* classes possesses the most of those five, both in number and degree, that man is entitled to most respect, even a Sūdra if he had entered the tenth decade of his age.

Way must be made for a man in a wheeled carriage, or above ninety years old, or afflicted with disease, or carrying a burthen ; for a woman ; for a priest just returned from the mansion of his preceptor ; for a prince, and for a bridegroom.

Among all those, if they be met at one time ; the priest just returned home and the prince are most to be honoured ; and of those two, the priest just returned, should be treated with more respect than the prince.'

VISIT WITH PRESENTS

Of the many unique customs prevalent among the Hindus, the one enjoining the visit to an individual with a present is perhaps the most common. There is an Indian proverb which says that 'One should not go to visit a king, a child, a pregnant woman, the preceptor and an image of God in a temple, empty-handed.' This custom is strictly adhered to at least by the majority of the Hindus even at the present day. When visiting children, sweets are generally taken and at times sugarcandy, as presents. Women in general and pregnant women in particular are visited with new cloth, saffron, flowers, fruits and betel-leaves with areca-nuts. When going to temples people take with them cocoanuts, fruits, flowers and *pan supari*. Lime fruits and gems are considered most suitable for presentation when visiting kings.

The reason why children should be visited with presents of sweets, etc., to them is simply this. Children are undeveloped and consequently could not understand the object of the visitor's visit to them; nor could they understand their visitor's love towards them in the abstract. Something material, tangible and visible is necessary to attract them to the intending visitor. Hence, from an ordinary worldly point of view, presents are to be taken when visiting children to attract them and this makes it possible to fondle them, resulting in the drawing out of affection between the visitor and the visited. Further, in this custom there is the germ of self-denial and attention to the benefit of others.

Pregnant women should be visited with presents for the reason that they have peculiar cravings for special eatables, fruits and things, when they are quick with child and this fact is recognized by one and all. Consequently when one goes a-visiting them, he carries things which he considers may be acceptable and welcome. Further, the very fact that they are going to usher into the world children who may perhaps prove—when they grow up to be men and women—greatest benefactors of humanity, has perhaps originated the custom. From this point of view a woman quick with child should be considered an object to show one's feelings of joy and expectation. Hence articles considered by the people to be suitable for use on happy occasions such as new cloths, fruits, flowers, betel-leaves with areca-nuts, vermilion, saffron, and so forth are taken to them as presents. Further it is believed by the Hindus that women when they are pregnant are under the special attention of a *dēvata* or deity who is always with her attending to the growth of the child in the womb. Hence what is considered a present to the woman is in reality a present to the *dēvata* and it is considered to be an act of great merit.

The Hindu scriptures say that a portion at least of God in His preservative aspect abides in kings. Hence the custom of carrying presents to the king and offerings to temples may be dealt with together. As has already been hinted at, this custom draws out the latent love in man, his patriotism to the country, his loyalty to the king and his devotion to God. Moreover, God is said to be the embodiment of love. The whole world is teeming with His love as evinced from the affection shown not only by men towards his kith and kindred, but also by the birds of the air, and the beasts of the woods towards their species and young ones. The leader elephant is ready to brave danger for the safety of the other weaker ones whom he loves by advancing in front of the herd. The strong wild goats lie in a circle around the herd to protect it from danger. As all these actions arise from love, it is but natural that man seeks for ways and means to draw out the love latent in him. How else could he do it but by taking such opportunities by the top ?

Precious stones were considered suitable presents to the kings, for the reason that the king possesses everything and consequently nothing that others could take with them as presents might be considered duly acceptable to him. Hence people take the best of gifts available, namely, gems.

As for taking lime fruits we can only say that among very ordinary presents such as fruits, the most pleasing to the sight and handy is the lime fruit and consequently is the gift resorted to by people not rich enough to take with them gems as presents to the king. In this connection it may be interesting to note that the *Report of the Madras Epigraphical Department* for the year 1910–11 (page 87), says that the copper-plate grants relating to Tirumalai Nāyak of Madura dated A.D. 1650–51 make mention of the applicants for the plates charter to have approached the kings, offering them *sēnisakkarai*, i. e., sugarcandy, as a *Nazzar*, which is still the orthodox etiquette observed in visiting high personages.

Preceptors should not be visited empty-handed because one seeks a *guru* to gain wisdom, and wisdom, pure and simple is the joy of giving and not grasping. A would-be disciple by taking presents to his preceptor shows that he is ready to impart to others the knowledge he may gain from him. Further from the highest philosophical standpoint presents to a preceptor means not ordinary worldly presents. Some disciples are said to take bundles of dried sacred twigs of the pipal tree as presents to their preceptors showing symbolically thereby that all his lower passions and desires, are ready to be cast in the fire of knowledge since knowledge supreme could be had only after bringing under perfect control passions like anger, desires, envy, etc., as laid down in the Hindu philosophical treatises.

YĀTHRA OR PILGRIMAGE

It is doubtful whether any nation attaches so much importance to *Yāthra* or Pilgrimage as do the Hindus. In bygone years when railways were unknown in the land, crowds of pilgrims used to leave their homes perhaps never to return after the obligatory *Dhānam* or gifts to the Brāhmans. They started at an hour declared auspicious by the village astrologer and after an offering perhaps of broken cocoanuts to the elephant-headed deity—Vināyakar—of the village and affectionate farewells to friends and relatives they commenced their long and wearisome journey to distant sacred places, temples or rivers. So toilsome indeed was the journey on pilgrimage that people used to associate it with any wearisome work or undertaking.

Why did the people undertake such a laborious journey, many even losing their lives owing to hardships, privations and change of climatic conditions? Not because they were credulous and superstitious, but because of the fact that they were sure that the risky journey on such pilgrimages was worth undertaking. What were the benefits the attainment of which tempted them to set their bodily pains and inconveniences at naught?

Barren women are said to become *enceinte*, if they in company with their husbands, visited certain places and lived there for some time. The beneficial results are perhaps due to the favourable climatic conditions or the peculiar property of certain springs, tanks or rivers due to the presence of minerals, remnants of medicinal plants or magnetism, for conception. Anyhow people did believe and do believe even now that a residence at particular places bestows on certain people certain beneficial physical results.

Monomaniacs and people said to be obsessed by evil spirits get cured of their disease by visiting certain places and remaining there for some time. Here too the beneficial results may be ascribed to the climatic and atmospheric conditions favourable for the cure of diseases of the nervous system. Even leprosy of a very virulent type is said to have been cured by a bath in certain springs, tanks and rivers or residence in a certain place for a period, and so it is no wonder that a spiritually inclined Hindu attached great importance to pilgrimage to holy places.

People who desire to attain enlightenment prefer to go to Gaya and meditate under the Bodhi tree, or the tree of wisdom, since Lord Buddha is said to have obtained enlightenment under it and consequently the locality surcharged with his magnetism is found to be highly favourable for the attaining of that calmness of mind, a *sine qua non* for every case of spiritual enlightenment. Similarly a Hindu temple, a Christian church and a Muhammadan mosque do each contribute tremendously for stirring up *Bhakti* or devotional emotion in consequence of the devotional magnetism of the devotees of years gone by with which each of such localities is surcharged and consequently sympathetic feeling of devotion is stirred up in persons resorting to them and who therefore feel benefited when returning to their abodes. This statement receives added strength not only by the expenses of the devotionally inclined, but also by the following historical incident of bygone days recorded in the history of King Bhōja. The incident itself in brief is as follows :—

King Bhōja was once returning to his capital after a prolonged hunting expedition completely worn out which

2

feeling was shared alike by one and all of his retinue. Afflicted with hunger and thirst they directed their steps towards a farm where they found its owner in a loft in the midst of a cucumber plantation.

Seeing the king and his followers approaching his farm in a jaded condition he cried out to them with unfeigned joy to eat the tender cucumbers and drink the water from the garden well to satisfy their hunger and allay their thirst. This he said when he was in the loft and when he came down from it he was altogether quite a different being and began to abuse the king and his followers for having trespassed on his farm like a mean-minded and selfish miser that he was! His highly charitable mood while on the loft was attributed to the magnetism radiating from and pervading the loft, of King Vikrama whose throne lay buried under the ground on which the loft was erected.

It seems Sri Rāma in his wanderings one day asked his brother Lakshmana as usual to hold his bow for a while. To his intense amazement he found Lakshmana replying that he was not his servant and that he might hold his bow instead. Carrying with him the clod of earth on which Lakshmana was standing when he gave the reply, Rāma continued his journey for a while. Arriving on the other bank of a river they had to cross, he again asked Lakshmana to hold his bow which he did most lovingly, dutifully and obediently! When Lakshmana was made to stand on the clod of earth he had brought and requested to hold Rāma's bow, he insolently replied that he was not to serve Rāma and Rāma was to serve him!

Another incident is that King Karikālchōḷa, whose fame is connected with the City of Conjeeveram, where in the Ēkāmbarēsvara temple is a sculptural representation of his, once rode on his state elephant into the forest near Trichinopoly when to his surprise a fat-looking cock attacked the elephant! Surprised at this extraordinary and unusual boldness of a tiny cock combating a huge elephant the king was induced to know the cause of it. Learning that it was due to the soil of the place, which made the inhabitants of the place so strong, he resolved upon a town being formed there which on this account was first named 'Kōzhiyūr' (*Kōzhi* being the Tamil name for cock) and this came to be known later on as 'Uraiyūr' (*Orthura Basileios Sornagos* of the Greeks).

Hence we may take it for granted that certain localities and certain individuals can and do exercise influence over others either for good or for evil and *Yāthras* prescribed by the ancients are really beneficial to people.

SŪRYANAMASKĀRAM OR PROSTRATION BEFORE THE SUN

No Hindu custom is considered so important as the one going by the name of *Sūryanamaskāram*. The custom though intended to worship the sun generally, the importance of the observance lies in the prostration or alternate standing and falling flat on the ground as implied in the name itself.

History tells us that the Āryan ancestors of the Hindus worshipped the sun as the creator, the nourisher and the destroyer of everything in the universe. Hindu *Upanishads* tell us that the sun is 'The-All' in the universe. Hence it stands to reason that the Hindus are expected to worship the sun in a befitting manner. But the custom of prostration needs examination and explanation.

Indian super-scientists were of opinion that the sun radiated a force which divided itself into seven kinds of forces symbolically represented as the seven horses of the Sun. These seven forces are of vital importance to men, animals and plants; and they radiate early in the morning very gently. The radiating force may be compared to the milk of animals when their young ones are very tender. Just as the milk thickens with the growth of the calf, these forces become stronger and stronger with the rising sun. There is this change not because the sun is sending out ever-changing forces, but because of the position of the earth with reference to the sun and the other planets.

The ancient sages had by their *Yōgic* powers found out the exact hours when the atmosphere and the magnetic conditions were most favourable for specific purposes. The early morning, the noon and the hour of sunset were considered by them most suitable for men to recoup and charge certain dynamos in their system, to wit, the mental and the will dynamos.

To control the mind and store the mental dynamo with the solar force, the body should not be very active. In fact it should be pretty sufficiently exhausted. With this end in view prostration is prescribed. Generally it may be mentioned that all customs requiring mental control require of men previous fast.

To create a receiver of the force the sun is visualized by imagination and to secure the concentration of the wandering and ever restless mind, certain *mantrams* or incantations are prescribed.

It is laid down by the wise that a strict observance of this custom of *Sūryanamaskāram* would confer on the observer extended vision. There is a reference in the *Report of the Epigraphical Department* for 1920-1921, page 115, to the *Sūryasataka* being engraved in the Kachchapēsvara temple at Conjeeveram. 'Mayūrakavi was a court poet, who flourished in the court of Harsha in the first half of the seventh century A.D. . . . His only work is the *Sūryasatakam*, which is also popularly known by the name of *Mayūrasatakam* . . . their literary merit coupled with the miraculous results which are alleged to have attended their composition, have secured for them great popularity among the orthodox. The author appears to have been suffering from blindness and to have been cured of his troublesome disease by composing these verses in praise of god Sūrya, so that even to-day these verses are used for purposes of *Pārāyanam* (i.e., devout recitations).'

There is also a proverb which means that 'THERE IS NO USE IN PERFORMING *Sūryanamaskāram* AFTER

THE SIGHT IS LOST.' What they actually meant was perhaps 'knowledge' and not the power of seeing simply. It is said that light is knowledge and darkness is ignorance. So this performance of *Sūryanamaskāram* is considered to be capable of bestowing on the observer of the custom supreme knowledge which means the knowledge of the end and aim of life.

Some believe that the prostration not only gives sufficient exercise for the man performing it, but it also serves the purpose of a valve in receiving the vital force and passing it on to the reservoir in the body.

PARTING WITH MONEY AFTER SUNSET

The reason why money should not be given after sunset may be considered highly interesting. An orthodox Hindu would not permit an iron article, money, etc., to be taken out of his house by others after sunset. The reason for this, so far as it is possible to be ascertained, appears, to be the belief that the invisible beings and forces contributing to the happiness and welfare of the inmates of a house, center round certain objects and household utensils after sunset and if the objects are taken away, the beings and forces are also carried away along with them, to enrich and benefit the individual carrying them off ever afterwards, subsequently. Hence the individual who parts with his money and other allied objects parts with them the beneficent entities and influences. This is still in vogue and the bridegroom's party take away any one of the iron articles from a bride's house on the eve of their departure after the marriage is over.

The Hindus believe that hosts of invisible beings dwell side by side with them in their houses, taking their places over certain places and objects. This fact is emphasized by the observance of certain ceremonials like the performance of *Srāddha* where these invisible entities are requested to go away from particular localities to enable them to perform their ceremonies in peace.

Some of these entities and forces are said to be in streets outside houses during the daytime and as soon as the night falls after sunset, they enter some one of the houses from the street to take rest during the night. Just as a benighted traveller would be filled with delight at the sight of a restaurant or hotel with lights burning and tables ready laid out, these benighted entities and forces of nature welcome a house kept tidy with lights burning. They readily enter it and if they find the people and accommodation suitable for them, they stay there permanently, making the inmates happy and prosperous by the influence radiating from them.

All good entities of the invisible world around us are said to love light, and abhor darkness. All bad and evil denizens of that world abhor light and take delight in darkness. A bat and an owl love to roam in darkness, while the other birds like the parrot seek their nest after sunset. A bat and an owl are birds of ill repute, said to be serving witches while the parrot and other similar birds that delight in light are said to serve the *dēvas* like *Manmatha* (Indian cupid) whose vehicle a parrot is said to be in the same way as the brāhmani-kite, peacock, swan, etc., are said to be the vehicles of Vishnu, the preservative aspect in the universe, Lord Subrahmanya, the second-born of Śiva and Pārvati representing wisdom, Brahma, the creative aspect and so on.

With this strong belief in the background, people take great care to have lights burning in shut up houses to prevent entities of evil repute from entering them and making them their permanent abodes.

The goddess Lakshmi is said to abide in money, flowers, betel-leaf, saffron, turmeric, the burning flame of a light and so on. If they are given to others during the daytime, the link connecting the entities presiding over them to their owners is not snapped by the effect of the solar light, and hence they return to their original abode before sunset, as if by instinct through this connecting link so to say; but if they were given after sunset the link is lost and the entities are in the position of children taken to other places while asleep and in course of time inured to their new surroundings and people benefiting them and enriching them by their radiating influences. This appears to be one of the chief reasons if not the chief reason for the reluctance of the Hindus to part with or lend certain objects to friends and others after the lights are lighted after sunset and nightfall.

In trying to understand the 'why' of the Hindu customs, one should bear in mind that they were originated by very great men among the forefathers of the Āryans and others and hence, they ought not to be lightly disposed of. We must remember the dictum 'THERE IS MUCH IN THE HINDU CUSTOM THAT WE ARE NOT AWARE OF.'

BRAHMACHĀRI'S FOOD

LOOKING back upon the old civilization yielding place to the new, we find this custom most prominent then almost disappearing now. In days gone by, Indian villages had knots of *Brahmachāri* youths chanting the *Vēdas* in the mornings and in the evenings and begging their food from door to door at noon and after sunset.

Till about the age of five, the Brāhmin male child should be fed and taken care of by their parents. At about the age of five, he is invested with the sacred string after *Upanayanam* or initiation ceremony. From that time forward, he is bound to shift for himself and not be a burden to his parents.

Every man has to pass through four *āsramas* (stages of life), viz., *Brahmachāri*—the stage in which he is supposed to walk in the path towards the knowledge of the root of all ; *Grihasta* or the householder ; *Vānaprasta* —a forest dweller and *Sanyāsi* who gives up everything. Of these the stage of a *Brahmachāri* is one in which one lives for all, since the burden of the *Vēdas* he is studying is intended to teach *that and that only*. As he lives for all, all are in duty bound to protect him, feed him and support him. Hence has arisen the custom of *Brahmachāris* living on the charity of others. Even a *Sanyāsi* has to live on the charity of others but he does not gather handfuls of food from different houses just as *Brahmachāris* do. He takes his meals in a single house to which he is invited. The reason for the difference is obvious. A real *Sanyāsi* is one who has given up everything. He should not seek for food. Only if he is offered food by a *Grihasta*, he may eat; else he has to starve. In fact a *Sanyāsi* should be above the bodily wants and sufferings. But the case of a *Brahmachāri* is different. He has not given up the world just as the *Sanyāsi* has done. He is storing knowledge to be utilized later on as a *Sanyāsi*. He has to become a *Grihasta* ere long. So he has to come to various people so that they might know him well and offer him perhaps a girl in marriage to enable him to become a *Grihasta*. This is probably the main reason for his begging handfuls of rice from several houses. instead of getting the same from a single house.

He might also beg his handfuls of rice with some other motive. He may not be willing to make a single family bear the burden of feeding him. Perhaps he knows the advantage of collecting by easy instalments, so that the giver or the givers may not at all feel the giving. Moreover as the lads live ordinarily in the same village, and as there may be more *Brahmachāris* than one in the same village, the system of collecting handfuls of rice from a number of houses is perhaps the best system to be adopted. If there are a number of *Brahmachāris* they might divide the number of houses in the village into as many blocks as there are *Brahmachāris*, so that each may have his block to obtain his food from.

Sons of rich parents following this custom do not indiscriminately go into any house in the village. They generally choose the houses of their relatives and friends. But a true *Brahmachāri* should not do this, but consider all houses alike and beg his food from them without any choice.

MARGOSA LEAF IN FRONT OF HOUSES

ONE of the most ordinary South Indian Customs is perhaps that in connection with the use of the margosa (*melia azadirachta*) leaves. It has been the popular belief from time inmemorial that evil spirits are scared away by the special properties possessed by the margosa leaf. When women and children start on a journey, a few margosa leaves are given to them or placed somewhere on their bodies securely. Evil spirits are generally supposed to possess only women and children and not strong-willed men. But children and weak women, armed with a few margosa leaves, are believed to be safe. The reason for this is not far to seek perhaps. Certain insects like the flies gather generally in unclean places and upon rotten things. Fine strong scents are abhorrent to them and so they run away from places where they are kept. Similarly the spirits good and evil are attracted and repelled by magnetism, animal and vegetable. The Indians believe that certain evil spirits are capable of creating death-dealing microbes in the human body and cause epidemics like small-pox, cholera, etc. But the presence of the margosa leaves perhaps nullifies their efforts in this direction and foiled in their attempts they go away perhaps. Whatever may be the properties of the margosa leaves, the people do believe that they have the power to shield them from harm from epidemics or at least to lessen their virulence.

In front of the houses whose inmates are laid up with small-pox, measles, etc., one might invariably see a bunch of margosa leaves thrust in the eves. Quantities of the leaves may also be seen scattered near and around the patients. Pregnant women and women in confinement are considered to be susceptible to the influence of bad spirits. Perhaps the magnetism, etc., emanating from them and the new-born babies are agreeable to them and consequently attract them in large numbers. So to scare away such evil spirits a bunch of margosa leaves is thrust in the eves of the roof directly in front of the house immediately after the confinement of a woman in a house.

Margosa tree was and is being considered to have excellent medicinal properties, may be evinced from the following popular story :—

Once there lived in a village a husband and a wife. The husband was about to start on a long journey but the wife did not like it and desired if possible to stop him from undertaking it. She consulted an old woman, a friend of hers. She advised her to obtain from her husband a promise that he would, on his way to the place of pilgrimage sleep only under tamarind (*tamarindus indica*) trees and on his return journey under margosa trees. The woman did obtain from her husband the said promise. The husband started on his journey and kept up his promise to his wife to sleep under tamarind trees. A few days' sleep under the tamarind trees made him very sick and so he had to give up his journey and turn homewards. Remembering the promise made to his wife he began to sleep under margosa trees on his return journey when lo ! in a few days he was cured of his illness !

The above story is of course intended to show the popular belief in the efficacy of the margosa tree in curing diseases, and it also shows the belief people had in the tamarind tree. They used to say that tamarind is to a house what the tiger is to the forest. It is considered to be such an injurious thing as to make a sickly man worse if possible.

Most people do not believe in superphysical beings like the evil spirits referred to above nor do they believe that they could create germs and microbes, the root causes of all epidemics and other diseases. But one and all do believe that the germs and microbes cause in human beings various diseases and that cholera, plague, small-pox and many other epidemics may be and are traced to them. Nowadays various drugs are being experimented upon by medical experts to find out their properties. As drugs that could destroy germs and microbes are valuable and as people of ancient days would not have placed so much confidence in the efficiency of margosa leaves, etc., if experience had not shown them that they were productive of good and beneficial results, margosa leaves deserve to be experimented upon.

The bark of the old margosa tree is said to possess excellent medicinal properties and physicians often administer its decoction or medicine in its decoction to effect certain cures in certain cases of fever and so on. The tender leaves are said to have the power to kill the worms in the stomach and the intestines. Consequently we may safely say that the leaves do possess germicidal properties.

A woman soon after delivery is susceptible to the attack of any disease and consequently every precaution should be taken to destroy microbes if any that may be brought into the house by men, animals and things. The margosa leaves, though they may not be able to destroy the microbes completely, appear at least to possess the properties of paralysing the activities of the germs causing contagious diseases like small-pox. Some even think that the smell of the margosa leaves prevents the breeding of the microbes and hence the evil is reduced to a minimum and the attack may not grow worse or virulent. The margosa leaves do possess some properties in the manner suggested above there is no gainsaying. People believe that the tamarind tree would enhance any disease while the margosa tree would cure even the worst type of sickness, if patients were brought near and kept there sufficiently long. Avenues and groves of margosa trees may be created near isolation hospitals and some patients kept near them or in them and the effect noted. Some wise men are of opinion that groves and avenues of certain trees should be near hospitals to make experiments. Patients suffering from fever, small-pox, etc., may be placed in buildings in the middle of the margosa groves, since it is found that the bark of this tree cures fever and checks the virulence of small-pox. Similarly a cocoanut grove may be made use of to experiment on men having weakened systems by the exhaustion of nerves, and a grove of Punga trees (*Pongamia glabra*), to cure lung diseases like consumption, asthma and so on.

The curative properties of plants should first be ascertained and patients should be placed in the atmosphere of such living plants as are supposed to have properties to cure particular diseases. It is also suggested that combined groves of trees of diverse kinds may be formed guided by the ingredients going to make up mixtures for various ailments.

KOḌUKKU NEEKKAL

Koḍukku Neekkal is another custom peculiar to the South Indian people. The corners of a towel or a cloth are given the name of *Koḍukku* and these at times owing to the careless shaking of cloths by people strike the eye of some one resulting in a kind of eye disease called by the people *Koḍukku.* Medicines like eye drops do not cure this disease and a peculiar custom is followed by the people to effect a cure and they say that the practice is generally efficacious and brings about the cure of the complaint. If by some accident or other, a boy or a girl or a man or a woman happen to suffer from this *Koḍukku-paḍal* as the disease is called in Tamil, then some member of the house, generally a woman, takes in a vessel some water steeped in turmeric and goes to seven houses successively one after another. As she should not open her mouth and talk, she simply stands there till the attention of the lady of the house is drawn to her. She would understand even from the vessel containing the turmeric water brought by the other women the purpose she had come for. If she does not, this woman with the turmeric water, by dumb shows points out her eye and the corner of her cloth thereby indicating the purpose she has come for. As this custom is most common, no difficulty is felt anywhere to achieve the end in view by the lady coming with the vessel of turmeric water. The lady of the house dips a corner of her cloth in the yellow water a few times after which the lady with the turmeric water goes to another house to have the process repeated there. After having gone to seven houses as described above and after having had the corners of the cloths worn by the ladies of those houses dipped in the turmeric water, the woman returns home. There the patient suffering from *Koḍukku* is made to stand in a corner of the courtyard where two roofs meet and goes by the name of *Kooḍu-Vōi-Moolai.* An old broom is then held from the corner of the roof and the turmeric water is made to fall through it. The patient suffering from *Koḍukku* washes his eye with the turmeric water falling through the old broom. This process is repeated a few days and then the patient is completely cured!

A good deal of this custom may appear absurd; yet experience has shown to the people that the practice produces beneficial results and so without caring to know whether the practice is absurd or not even some of the educated sceptics who had the misfortune to suffer from this complaint of *Koḍukku* have submitted to this treatment. Could any rational explanation be drawn out of them? Turmeric has healing properties is known to all. If slaked lime happens to come into contact with the eye or any other delicate part of the body it is the practice to apply turmeric water freely to counteract the evil effect of chunam or slaked lime. Children suffering from sore-eyes in villages are provided with pieces of cloths dyed with saffron or turmeric to wipe their eyes with. So the saffron water might play a very prominent part in healing the complaint of the eye due to *Koḍukku.* As regards the portion of the custom relating to the corners of the cloths and the saffron water being dipped into with them by the ladies, we can only speculate as to the probable reason for it. The cloths worn by men and women are saturated with their magnetism. As they are being overcharged every moment, a portion of the magnetism in the cloth is always escaping into space through the corners of the cloths worn by men and women. The dipping of the corners of the cloths into the saffron water charges it perhaps with the escaping magnetism and this coming into contact with the magnetism left in the eye of the patient by *Koḍukku-paḍal*, perhaps neutralizes its evil effects. The complaint due to *Koḍukku* is not cured with eye-drops, etc. So it gives room to say that the ailment is not due so much to the injury in the eye but to the magnetism left in it by the *Koḍukku-paḍal*. It may be asked pertinently by people conceding this as to why a number of people should be approached to steep the saffron water with the outgoing magnetism from their bodies through the corners of their cloths. In reply we can but state that it might be probable that different people throw out different kinds of magnetism and to neutralize one kind a special kind is perhaps needed. That kind may not be had from one. So if a number of people are approached, the kind of magnetism required was perhaps obtained.

As regards the use of the broom we may say that that too might have some share in the cure of the ailment due to *Koḍukku*. The earth is charged with the magnetism of different sorts and conditions of people. The broom sweeping the ground is perhaps charged with diverse kinds of magnetism. When saffron water overcharged with the personal magnetism of seven ladies who dipped the corners of their cloths into it is poured through the broom, the magnetism in it was perhaps carried down by the saffron water, which, when made use of by the patient, secured for him freedom from ailment. Further cumulative thought force is very powerful. So if seven or more ladies strongly think that they are aiding in the cure of a particular ailment and dip the corners of their cloths in the saffron water, the saffron water becomes perhaps a very powerfully magnetized water.

The reason why the lady going with the saffron water should not talk is perhaps difficult even to speculate upon. She is perhaps trying to aid in magnetizing the saffron water powerfully by her power of concentrating the will on it. If she were permitted to talk and say about the object of her visit, she might be led to talk on other things also. Then the oneness of purpose may be destroyed which may perhaps nullify all the other efforts.

CONTAGIOUS DISEASES

CONTAGIOUS diseases that are looked upon as the result of the susceptibility of the human system to the attack of germs and microbes, in countries other than India, are looked upon as the work of certain deities by the Hindus especially of South India. It is the inborn belief of a real Hindu that every tree, plant and animal may be influenced by invisible intelligences with very fine invisible bodies going by the names spirits or *dēvatas*. Some of these *dēvatas* are beneficent and some are in malevolent. The beneficent deities are by nature quite incapable of doing any harm. If at all they influence human beings, it would be only to do them good. Taking for instance a dog that has come into a house, it plays with the children and gives delight to them. If a scorpion comes into a house it stings the unwary children and causes them excruciating pain. Similarly the good *dēvatas* attracted to houses make the children healthy, and cheerful even by their very presence, whereas the evil *dēvatas* create by their presence in the houses the epidemic germs that attack children and others causing them trouble unbearable.

The dog or the scorpion causes joy or misery not at all knowing what either of them does. It is in the nature of the dog to love children, play with them and make them happy. It is the nature of the scorpion to sting and thereby cause pain. Exactly similar to the actions of these creatures are the doings of the *dēvatas*. Good *dēvatas* influence the growth of the children physically, mentally and morally by their mere presence in a house.

Just as rotten fruits, etc., breed worms, etc., in them, the bad *dēvatas* breed out of them microbes of epidemics to trouble children and others.

People believe that those *dēvatas* are simply having their play and enjoyment at the expense of the poor afflicted children and others. People troubled with a nest of ants try not to anger the insects but to leave them alone if possible waiting for the suitable opportunity to get rid of them. Similarly people whose children are attacked with small-pox, measles, etc., try not to anger the *dēvatas* behind those diseases but to propitiate them. Medicines and drugs if administered, are considered to displease the *dēvatas* who accordingly make the disease more virulent. Hence people are terribly afraid to administer medicines to children, lest they should unwittingly provoke the *dēvata* playing and enjoying in the house and incur his or her displeasure. People have found out by experience that gingelly oil heated to fry mustard seed in it, increases the virulence of the small-pox. Flowers, scents, etc., also make the patients worse. So when there is a case of small-pox in a house no gingelly oil should be heated to fry mustard to flavour vegetables with. No inmate of the house should anoint his or her body with gingelly oil. No shaving is permitted in a house containing a case of small-pox.

Sexual intercourse of people in the house would be the cause of greatest injury to the patient. Hence young men and women should be made to be very careful and guarded, not only to save the patient from harm but also to save him from loss of eyesight, considered most common after a virulent attack of small-pox, and perhaps even death.

People of the present time may not believe in the existence of the *dēvatas* and in their ability to produce microbes causing and spreading death-dealing epidemics like small-pox, measles, etc. But they do believe in the fact that germs and microbes are the causes of the epidemics. The ancient customs have behind them certain aspects of truth and usefulness. Gingelly oil and mustard seed fried together are known to increase the virulence of small-pox and measles. Experiences of years have taught the people this fact and they firmly believe in it. A visit to any village infested with small-pox or measles would surely convince any one of the truth of what has been set forth above. Such being the case the reason for this long-standing belief must be enquired into. Scientists say that certain minute fungus germs, the seeds of which are in the air, attack vegetables and make them rot and decompose. So why should there be not microbes living in the cells, etc., of human body that gain strength with the smell emanating from gingelly oil, mustard, flowers, etc. ? These perhaps with their increased strength increase the virulence of the disease.

Most people who revere the deity behind diseases like small-pox do not know anything about the theory of germs and microbes that cause epidemics and many other diseases. They simply and perhaps blindly believe in a deity behind the disease that is susceptible to feelings of emotion like anger, pleasure, etc. So they offer to the deity in question deep obeisance and profound reverence. They, in fact, conduct themselves exactly as they would do if there happened to be a great and holy personage dwelling in the house temporarily.

A particular period of time is patiently waited to elapse even after the disease is cured and then the deity is properly worshipped and sent off in a manner supposed to be befitting her dignity. One noteworthy feature in the observance of this custom is that people are not allowed to enter the house in which a patient is laid up with small-pox, measles, etc., freely, nor are people ready to do so. This is perhaps due to the fear on the part of the relatives of the sick that the people coming in might be impure and consequently by their approach near the patient increase the virulence of the disease. It might also be due to the fear on the part of the strangers that they might get the contagion. Be what it might, a sort of quarantine and isolation is ensured by the strict observance of this custom of restricting the visit of strangers to the patients. Another noteworthy feature is that rice, etc., are not to be bestowed in charity from an infected house. This is perhaps due to the fear that the beggars might be impure or it may also be with the intention that the contagion may not be carried through grain, food, etc., bestowed in charity At any rate there is a safeguard against the disease spreading to others by this practice of not bestowing anything in charity from infected houses.

After a patient is cured and the scabs formed have fallen off which generally takes place on the twenty-first day after the attack, the goddess is not sent off for some days more. The reason for this is not far to seek. The people knew that the people in a house not affected by the disease were not immune from the danger of an attack of the disease till a particular period of time is passed. It is known that this disease small-pox has remained in a house for a pretty long period attacking first one member and then a few days after he or she is cured another member, and so on. Though two or more people in a family may be laid up with small-pox, measles, etc., it generally happens most frequently that one member is completely cured before another member is attacked and laid up in bed. The diet prescribed to the patient goes to show that the people knew how the disease originated and how certain things like chillies are injurious and how tender cocoanuts, etc., are beneficial to those suffering from this epidemic. The opinion of people having the experiences of centuries behind them should not be brushed aside without careful examination and therefore particulars about the primitive customs are very valuable.

MAṄGAḶA VĀDYAM OR PIPING

IT is one of the many peculiar Hindu customs that all auspicious rites and ceremonies are heralded and followed by what is called the *Maṅgaḷa Vādyam*, which is but the chorus of music made by a piper, a drummer and a man who keeps tune using a *Jālra* or two sonorous metallic discs. The rich and poor alike observe this custom and consequently many undergo training in this art from a particular community (barbers now-a-days taking to it in some places) and earn their livelihood.

This is in fact a profession which gives a good income provided the piper becomes an expert and specially efficient. Many famous pipers have come and gone in Southern India who were considered to be geniuses in the art. For a day's engagement, there have been occasions when two hundred and even three hundred rupees have been paid to them. As in every vocation in life, there are also men of low attainments, medium attainments, and experts in this particular line also. As this *Vādyam* is a *sine qua non* on all auspicious occasions none of them fail to get remuneration according to their deserts.

This is one of the time-worn customs of the Hindus. Every temple considered to be in well-to-do, though not in affluent circumstances, had a set of these musicians attached to it.

Music, according to the nature of the tune played, can either quieten down or rouse the passions in men and animals. In ancient times, music was introduced in temples to soothe the devotees and thus to help them to feel the presence of God in a calm attitude of mind. This aspect is supported by the institution of vestal virgins attached to Hindu temples, who by the purity of life led, became channels for the flow of influences affecting devotees, in those bygone days.

When the soothing influence of music is recognized, then its introduction during the performance of auspicious rites and ceremonies would become intelligible.

The ancient Hindus had recognized the power of mental discharge of men as thoughts. In those days there were many strong-willed but easily excited people, since they were novices in *Yōga* who had not brought their passions and emotions under control. Further there may be others not having very friendly feelings towards the people for whom the ceremonies are arranged. These, by their emotions and thoughts, counteract the force of love and good-will directed towards the party. So music of a particular nature was resorted to to keep all people in a soothing temper to give the party their cumulative blessings and good-will, in those days. All these principles appear to have been lost sight of now-a-days ! ! !

MARRIAGE PRELIMINARIES

UNLIKE the practice in vogue in other countries, marriage of Indian youths and maidens is arranged and brought about by their elders to wit parents or guardians. The custom of betrothal as well as the going through of the preliminary formalities followed in South India is perhaps unique. Parents and guardians of marriageable youths and maidens meet and have a talk. They exchange horoscopes of boys and girls and go to consult astrologers about the suitability or otherwise of the marriage with reference to the position, etc., of the planets noted in them at the time of their birth. The horoscopes are compared to see in how many of the ten aspects laid down that they suit each other. The ten aspects are (1) Suitability regarding the day; (2) Suitability regarding the asterism; (3) Suitability regarding the *Ganam* such as human, *dēva* or *rākshasa* they are classed under in regard to the asterism they were born under; (4) Suitability regarding the *Mahēndram* or the relationship arising out of the planets the boy and girl were born under; (5) Suitability arising out of *Yōni* or genital organ which each asterism is assigned and which goes by the name *Yōnipporutham.* Certain *Yōnis* only could suit, for example, the *Yōni* of the elephant and lion cannot suit while the same *Yōni* for both would suit. Besides the five noted above there are six more suitability tests the horoscopes are subjected to, namely:—*Rāsipporutham, Rāsi Adipathipporutham, Vasyapporutham, Rajjupporutham, Vēdaipporutham,* and *Nādipporutham.* In addition to the above suitability tests there are also other tests to which the horoscopes are subjected to. It is impossible to find two horoscopes suiting each other satisfying all the conditions. If at least the most important conditions and some of the other conditions are satisfied, then the astrologers declare that the horoscopes suit and the marriage between the youth and the maiden may be celebrated. The Brāhmins trace their descent from one or other of certain specified *Rishis* and a boy and girl in that line of descent should not marry.

When the parties agree that the marriage between the boy and the girl may be celebrated, they proceed to the discussion of the terms of the marriage. That is they discuss and settle what each side should do to the other side by way of gifts of cash, silver and brass vessels, jewellery and so on. Then they exchange *pan supari* and the function goes by the name *Nichyathāmbulam*. Subsequently, on a day, previously fixed as convenient for both parties, the bride's party proceed to the residence of the bridegroom's party with two or three brass plates containing sugar-candy, sugar, bananas, betel, arecanuts, flowers, sandal paste, saffron, etc., and are received by the other party. Then the villagers as many of them as possible are invited. After they are all assembled, the bride's party give out that they have resolved to give the girl so and so to the boy so and so and the boy's party accept the offer. The terms of the marriage too are given out by the parties and accepted. Cash payments if agreed upon may then be made by one party to the other. Then fruits, sugar, sandal paste, *pan supari*, etc., are distributed to those present and a feast is held to which not only the boy's party, but also the villagers either all or a select few are invited. The leader of the boy's party is presented with a pair of new cloths as a mark of respect returned.

As the date for the celebration of the marriage is decided upon at the time of meeting prior to the distribution of fruits, etc., and the feast, the bride's party then return home to make the necessary preparations and arrangements. On the day previous to the one fixed for the wedding ceremony to take place the bridegroom is taken in procession to the house kept ready for his reception. The bridegroom's party occupy that house till the marriage ceremony is over and they are sent off by the bride's party.

At the time of the *Nichithārtham* function the bridegroom's party should give for the use of the bride a pretty good cloth to wear with half a yard of petticoat cloth. No female cloth should be presented without the addition of a petticoat cloth on any occasion whatever.

As soon as the bridegroom is received in the house provided for his use after due procession, the gentleman who is to give away the bride, presents to the bridegroom a pair of new cloth wearing which and helped by his father or in the absence of one by some elderly member, he has to go through a ceremony called *Vratham.* As soon as the *Vratham* is finished the bridegroom pretends that he is on his way to Benares. Then the bride's party or rather the one who is to give away the bride meets him and requests him not to go to Benares. He offers to give his daughter or ward as the case may be to him in marriage with a view to make him settle and lead a family life. The bridegroom of course embraces the offer and throws away the paraphernalia of a pilgrim. He is then taken to the bride's house and there the girl is gifted over to him. Then with the assistance of the family priest he marries the girl received by him as a gift, after going through certain formalities and marriage rites and ceremonies. When once they are married by the observances of the prescribed rites, nothing can part them and they are man and wife for life. Herein lies the difference between the marriage tie of a Hindu and that of one belonging to any other nation. So a Hindu marriage is a sacrament and not a contract. The other nations, for example, the Europeans can sever their wedding ties with the aid of a divorce court, but a Hindu can never do it. The bridegroom marries his wife in the presence of Agni—the God of fire and various other *dēvas* whose presence is invoked and who are supposed to be present at the time when the marriage ceremony is taking place. So no human being has power to sever the marriage tie tied in the presence of the divine beings. Further the bridegroom takes a solemn promise that he would take care of her for life. The reason why a large number of people are invited to be present at the time of the wedding is perhaps to make it impossible for the bridegroom to deny having married the girl if he were tempted to do so. Further, daily procession and if that be not possible, at least the procession on the last day of the marriage, makes known even to those not present at the time when the marriage knot was tied, the fact that they were man and wife for evermore.

Another practice followed is the presentation of cloths to the father-in-law and the mother-in-law both by the bride and the bridegroom's party. After the marriage is over at the end of four days, the bridegroom and his party are sent off with food, cakes, etc., furnished in plenty to be taken away with them to be made use of on the way. It should not be forgotten that the marriage ceremony takes place in the bride's house and not in the house of the bridegroom. The bride's party should look to the comfort and convenience of every one of the bridegroom's party during the four or five days of the marriage ceremony during which time they are their guests. Morning breakfast, midday meal, tiffin and night meal should be provided in a decent scale to the bridegroom's party by the bride's party.

This custom is the one followed by the Brāhmins of South India. The other castes may have customs entirely different, but the basic principle that the Hindu marriage is a sacrament and not a contract remains all the same.

UDAKASĀNTHI, I. E., AUSPICIOUSNESS THROUGH WATER

Of the innumerable customs of the Hindus, especially of the Brāhmins of Southern India, the purification of body with water made holy or in other words highly magnetized by the cumulative force of incantations recited by the priests and Brāhmins versed in the science and art, is perhaps one oft resorted to. No ceremony however ordinary it might be, is observed by a Hindu without having first bathed in cold water. In fact, physical purity should precede all performance of religious rites and ceremonies. A Hindu never begins his *Pooja* or worship of any deity without bathing. During new moon days a Hindu should offer libations to his *Pitris* or manes of the departed relatives. He would never perform this without bathing immediately before beginning it. Similarly, bathing is commonly resorted to to obtain physical purity. But the popular belief is that mere ordinary water may remove only physical impurities, adhering to the body but not the magnetic impurity. If magnetic impurities are to be removed, then magnetized water should be made use of. This water not only removes the physical impurities, but it removes magnetic impurities as well. To charge water with magnetism certain incantations are prescribed. If a Brāhmin desires to occupy a new house or a house recently vacated by some one, he would not do it without first demagnetizing the whole house, or in other words, he would remove the impure magnetism clinging to the house by sprinkling water specially magnetized by a process going by the name *Punyahāvāchanam*. Ordinarily, if the water is to be but slightly magnetized only one Brāhmin recites the incantation to charge the water placed before him in a vessel with *Dharba* grass, mango leaves and a cocoanut over it. He keeps touching the vessel either with his hand or with a few *Dharba* grass held in his hand.

When the recital of the *Japam* or incantation is over, the water is taken out and made use of. If the house or a particular room or rooms in it are to be demagnetized, the magnetized water is sprinkled everywhere with the mango leaf. To purify personal magnetism a spoonful of the magnetized water is swallowed and a quantity of it is sprinkled over the body. If it is deemed that a large quantity, say a big pot of water, is to be magnetized, then a number of persons take part in the recital of the *mantrams* or the incantations, all keeping the vessel containing the water to be mesmerized in touch through a tuft of *Kusa* grass held in their hands. The pot containing the water to be magnetized is decorated with mango leaves, saffron, sandal paste, etc., and the presence of Varuṇa—the God of Water—is invoked there with proper rites. The pot itself is placed on a dais of paddy or rice surrounded on all sides with *Kōlam* or floor decoration with rice flour. The occasions when magnetized water is in need are many. *Upanayanam* or thread-wearing ceremony, marriage ceremony, nuptials, *Seemantham* ceremony, *Punyahāvāchanam* after child-birth are occasions when magnetized water is needed. The boy to be invested with the sacred thread is made to bathe in the magnetized water before investiture. Similarly on other occasions also referred to above, the magnetized water is made use of to bathe the people in. The water magnetized during the *Punyahāvāchanam* after confinement is made use of, not only to demagnetize the house and the room the child was born in, but also to purify the mother, the baby and the father as well as others who had occasion to remain close to the mother and the new-born babe.

It is a fact acknowledged by all that water dissolves a large number of substances. Such being the case we may presume that it could dissolve fine matter surcharged with magnetism. The human eye and the human will magnetize certain kind of fine matter in space and drive them to any required place. In the *Udagasānthi Japam* or the process of magnetizing water, the eye and the will power of people engaged in the operation magnetize a large quantity of fine matter in space and drive the same inside the vessel containing water to be magnetized. The water of course readily absorbs the magnetized matter and thus becomes highly charged. This is perhaps the explanation that could be offered to people requiring the same. The custom of purification by the use of magnetized water is observed in case of pollutions of all kinds. If any one dies in a house, a ceremony called *Subhasweekaranam* is observed. Then also the purification with magnetized water is resorted to. The birth of a child gives pollution to some of the relatives of the parents of the child born. Similarly death of an individual gives pollution to some of his relatives. In all such cases the ceremony of purification by magnetized water is resorted to. What has been set forth above is the custom among the Brāhmins only and not generally among other castes.

CHAUḶAM OR SHAVING

LIKE the Christian baptism the Hindus have unique religious ceremonies for their children. As soon as a child is born in a Hindu family, it is incumbent on the parents that they perform four among several other ceremonies for them. These are (1) *Jātakarma* (casting the horoscope); (2) *Nāma karma* (name giving); (3) *Annaprāsana* (giving the first solid food); and (4) *Chauḷa* (shaving). Of these the fourth is the *Chauḷa* ceremony.

No true Hindu, unless he be a *Sanyāsin* (ascetic), should have his whole head shaved, nor should a child have long hair growing on the whole head unless it is a female child.

As soon as a male child grows to a particular age, say five, the parents consult the *Pañchāṅgam* (Hindu almanac) and with the assistance of the *Purōhit* (the family priest) select an auspicious day for the ceremony. The services of a piper with his assistants, the drummer, etc., are secured since every auspicious ceremony should have music performed by these. Certain rites are to be gone through and the father of the child is supposed to shave his son for the first time. As a razor in the hand of an inexperienced father, especially when it is sharp, must prove dangerous if put to its legitimate use he simply cuts a hair or two repeating certain *mantrams* and entrusts his child's head and perhaps its safety and solidarity to the barber, an expert in his art.

The portion of a garden overgrown with weeds is the portion not to be made use of. The growth of hair in one's body may be compared to the growth of weeds in a field. Scientists tell us that the sympathetic system is more developed in women than in men and the cerebro-spinal system is more developed in men than in women. Hence it may be inferred that the brain and the nervous system generally are made use of by men more than by women ordinarily. The brain centres below the crown are used to a greater extent than the centres at the back. So men have their crowns shaved while women grow the hair on the head to indicate the use or otherwise of the portions of the brain.

A *Grihasta* shaves off the hair from every part of the body excepting the forearms, eye-brows and the tuft of hair which is considered to be an essential thing for performing certain religious ceremonies, especially the rites for the dead. Whiskers and moustaches are considered undesirable to have when performing important religious rites.

Sanyāsins shave off the hair from the whole surface of the head and the chest since they are supposed to make use of all centres in the brain including the *Yōga* centres controlling the nervous system at the back.

Ascetics and *Rishis* grow hair over all parts of the body since they are almost dead to the world and consequently no part of the body is to be made use of by them when strictly considered.

DAMPATIS, I.E., HUSBAND AND WIFE

THE word *Dampati* means a husband and his wife, is known to one and all among the Hindus. But its significance, both religious and spiritual, is known to very few only. The moment the marriage knot is tied after the performance of the enjoined marriage rites, they become partners for life and the tie can be broken only by the death of one of them. Thus the Hindu marriage is a sacrament and not a contract as it is in other countries.

It is laid down in the Hindu *Dharma Sāstras*, that the ceremonials observed by a husband without the co-operation of his wife would be null and void. Hence an orthodox Hindu performs all ceremonies in company with his wife. If he goes on a pilgrimage, he takes his wife with him. If he performs the *Srāddha* for his *Pitris* (manes), his wife co-operates with him and helps him. If he bestows gifts on others, his wife joins him in giving away the gift by pouring a spoonful of water on the article held by her husband. In giving away a daughter in marriage, his wife must join him in the observances of the formalities attached to it; else the gift is valueless. Some people consider it a sin to feed a Brāhmin widower on certain occasions. Why is so much importance attached to the observances of and participations in religious observances by Hindu *Pampatis?* A man by himself is considered to be an imperfect being lacking that which is found in the other sex. He is just as a watch or any machinery that cannot be in working order if a part of it is missing. Hence the observances of religious rites and ceremonies by a man in the absence of his wife would be like trying to set in motion a machinery lacking in a part.

The sages of old who had knowledge of the working of forces set in motion by the observances of ceremonials, laid down principles, which if strictly followed, would make the ceremonials really effective. People in olden days had implicit faith in the sages who laid down rules for them to follow and hence did exactly as they were bidden to do and were none the worse for it.

Science tells us that a union of the positive and negative electricity is essential to emit a spark. Either kind of itself could effect nothing. Having this as the basis, experts in *Yōga* opine that for the vivifying of certain centres in the human body forces from both sexes, male and female, should be utilized. So after all, we have the explanation that a husband and his wife wholly devoted to each other, one living for and in another, become a mighty pivot to move anything on. Most of the *Dampatis* of ancient days were such and consequently were able to achieve great things. Further people who propitiated them and worshipped them were the better for their act, since they drew upon them from those *Dampatis* mighty influences which they would otherwise be unable to do.

Like most of the customs, this fine custom too has been ignored and, if at all observed anywhere, it is done in a manner ineffectual since the observer and the *Dampatis* are both unfit for the generation and direction of the influence as expected by or from them.

MĀLAI-MĀTRAL, I.E., THE EXCHANGE OF GARLANDS

It has been the immemorial custom among the Hindus that the bridegroom and the bride should be carried on the shoulders of their respective maternal uncles to exchange garlands of flowers on their necks, prior to the commencement of the regular marriage ceremony after the betrothal and on the three or four succeeding days. The bride and the bridegroom wear each on their necks two garlands. The respective uncles carrying them on their shoulders, bring them face to face near each other and the husband takes off from his neck one garland and garlands his betrothed with it. The bride then takes a garland from her neck and garlands her betrothed husband. This process is repeated thrice. This custom varies slightly with certain communities of the Hindus.

A community of Hindu people observe this custom, the bride and the bridegroom sitting or standing in front of each other. The custom of maternal uncles carrying the bride and the bridegroom on their shoulders to have their garlands exchanged is perhaps confined to the Brāhmins and the Kōmuṭis for the reason that the marriage of their girls takes place when they are very young, or, in other words, when they are about nine or ten years old. In other castes this practice is not followed for the obvious reason that the brides are generally girls who have attained puberty and the custom is not desirable to be followed in their case in consequence.

The Hindu youth is supposed to marry not with a

view to satisfy his carnal appetite, but with the definite aim of performing religious rites in company with his wife for the spiritual evolution of both. In fact, a wife is said to be a *Saha Dharma Chārini* which means the lady who performs the duty enjoined in company with her husband.

The observances of religious rites develops spirituality in the observers, both men and women. Like the sacred thread worn by the Brāhmins, these garlands symbolize spirituality. A husband by putting one of his two garlands, on the neck of his would-be wife, bestows on her a half of his spiritual force, and she repeating the process in her turn shares hers with him. This is the main end and aim to attain which all the subsequent rites are observed to be continued thereafter day after day till perfection in evolution is attained in both, taking many births even if need be as husband and wife.

The ancient Hindu custom of *Sati* had its origin perhaps from this. The husband when he dies waits for his wife in the next super-physical world. If she were to wait to caste off the fleshy body to join her husband on the other side by the natural process of death, it would take a long time and the husband would be kept waiting unnecessarily in a world perhaps uncongenial for him. Hence the ancient wise had discovered a plant, the juice of which when mixed with sandal paste and smeared over the body made the body insensible to the burning sensation and the wife wakes to find herself in company with her husband on the other side of death without having in the least felt the agonies of death in being burnt alive by having become a *Satī*. They then go together into the heaven world or *Swarga* to dwell there for a time and come back again to this world to continue the work of evolution. Thus we see in the plan laid down by the wise men of old that two souls drawn together by love real and sincere do not part till both reach the level at the same time. This idea is conveyed in the Hindu marriage ceremonials and the Hindu marriage itself is therefore considered a sacrament and not a contract as it is understood to be among certain peoples of the West as well as of the East.

A WIFE TO EAT AFTER HER HUSBAND

CONTRARY to the custom in vogue in other countries, the Hindu marriage is a sacrament and not a contract between the husband and the wife. When once this idea is grasped the duties devolving on the wife, so far as her husband is concerned, would become intelligible. She is expected to be the right half while the husband represents the left of a whole individual. In fact most of the important Hindu ceremonies are to be performed by an individual in company with his wife, if at all they are to be productive of effective results. There are certain ceremonies, for example, the tenth day ceremony for the dead that cannot be performed without the company of the wife of the man performing them.

A wife is called the *Saha Dharma Chārini* in Sanskrit which means the joint observer of the religious rites and ceremonies. The husband and the wife are considered to be one soul functioning in two bodies, one helping and enriching the other.

A study of the human system tells us that there are two systems of nerves in our body—the cerebro-spinal system and the sympathetic system. The former consists of the nerves of the brain and the spinal cord, while the latter system regulates the bodily functions of organs such as circulation and respiration. In man, the cerebro-spinal system is fully developed while in a woman the sympathetic system is emphasised. For *Yōga* and other ways of spiritual progress, the cerebro-spinal system is utilized. For the upkeep of the body the sympathetic system is important. In the absence of the former the latter would be non-existent and *vice versa*. Hence one must nourish the other system. Generally, the cerebro-spinal system is considered to be more important than the sympathetic system, being the one made use of for spiritual evolution considered to be the *summum bonum* of human existence. Hence it should be taken care of first. So a husband symbolizing the former system is nourished first and the wife is left what is not wanted for the husband to live upon.

The ordinary reason perhaps is that the husband by his practice of meditation and severe austerities has become a store house of magnetic force. While he is taking his meals, the plate or the leaf used with the food left in it is perhaps highly magnetized being saturated with his magnetism.

So by partaking of the food from the husband's leaf a wife absorbs into her system her husband's forcible magnetism and thus becomes purer. Further this magnetism if absorbed by other animals, might prove injurious to them, but a wife inured to her husband's magnetism would surely be the better for absorbing it into her system. This fact may be noticed in a family where the members are inured to the magnetism of the several members.

NALAṄGU, I.E., A DAMPATI AT PLAY

PERHAPS one of the most common of the Hindu customs is that going by the name *Nalaṅgu* performed generally during the evenings when a marriage ceremony is taking place for four days. The marriage is supposed to be performed by the bride's father and the bridegroom and his relatives are in the position of guests.

Every morning the bride's people bring to the quarters assigned for the bridegroom and his people cakes in new vessels which are to be gifts to the bridal pair. Then the relatives of the bridegroom perform the function of *Nalaṅgu* to the bride's people who brought them cakes for breakfast. This goes by the name *Sambandi Nalaṅgu.*

In the evenings, the bride and the bridegroom sit for *Nalaṅgu.* The function itself is rather unique and deserves examination. The bride and the bridegroom are seated opposite to each other on mats spread on the floor in the marriage *pandal.* The bridegroom stretches out his legs and the bride rubs over it turmeric paste. Then the bride stretches out her feet and the husband repeats the process in his turn.

Then the bride takes in her two hands rice coloured yellow, and after waving it round her husband's head scatters it away. This process is then repeated three times by the husband also in his turn. He too takes handfuls of coloured-rice and scatters it over and about his wife having first waved it round her head.

Then a crisp preparation from black gram called in Tamil *Appaḷām* is waved and broken over the head of the husband by the wife and then over the wife's head by the husband. Then when the bridal pair are engaged in a kind of ball play, the ladies assembled sing songs helped by the pipers who are ready there throughout, with their instrumental music. Then the bridal pair are seated side by side and ladies take *Hāratti* (waving before them a liquid mixture of turmeric and slaked lime) to cast off the evil from the evil-eye. Then *pan supari*, sandal, fruits, flowers, etc., are freely distributed to the ladies assembled.

The simplest explanation that can be given for this custom is perhaps the desire of the originators to bring the newly married couple nearer each other so that they might shake off their shyness and get accustomed to each other. The sandal paste, the saffron paste, etc., are only means to effect the above purpose. Further, sandal, saffron, flowers, coloured-rice, etc., are all symbolical of auspiciousness and consequently the free and abundant use of them indicates the joy felt by every one assembled there. Moreover, when a large number of ladies have come for the marriage, and when they are sumptuously fed with rice preparations, it goes without saying that they should have some recreation to pass their time. What other recreation but the one in which the bridal pair form the central figure would be most acceptable to the guest and highly gratifying to the host? The piper is engaged and work should be given him. So his services are utilized by the ladies to supplement their vocal songs.

The scattering of the yellow rice and the breaking over the heads of the thin and crisp cake *Appaḷām* are perhaps intended to propitiate the invisible beings supposed to surround newly married couple. They may also symbolize plenty for the bride and the bridegroom.

MARRIAGE PROCESSION

PROCESSION of the bridal pair along the main streets of the village is one of the customs peculiar to the Hindus. Not only the husband and the wife newly joined in wedlock are carried round the village in a palanquin or a car or on elephant's backs in *howdahs* or on horsebacks, but also *Brahmachāris* and girls who have attained puberty are to follow this time-worn custom, the former on the fourth day of the ceremony, called *Danḍuneer* and the latter after she bathes at the expiry of the three days after her first menstruation.

The palanquin or the car stops in front of each of the houses in the village. The lady inmate of the house or her daughter, comes out with a dish of turmeric water mixed with lime, and a cocoanut, plantain fruits, or *pan supari*. She first presents the occupants of the palanquin or the car with any one of the three items mentioned above and then casts off the effect of the evil-eye by waving the mixture of turmeric and lime by the side of the palanquin. This process is repeated at each and every one of the houses, the relatives of the occupant of the car or palanquin putting into the dish of the mixture emptied, some cakes, a fruit, sugar or *pan supari*. Further, all people in the street are given sandal paste, flowers, fruits and *pan supari*.

In the case of the procession of the girl who had bathed after her first menstruation, she is invited inside certain houses and there she is offered milk and fruit. After partaking of these she comes out and gets into the palanquin or the car to dismount again to repeat the process in many other houses.

The custom, fantastic as it may appear to be, is based on certain principles. In bye-gone days the civilization was quite different to that in vogue at the present time. In European countries the marriage is a contract and not a sacrament as it is with the Hindus. There the signatures of the contracting parties, namely, the husband and the wife are taken, and the contract is further attested by witnesses. Even then we have heard of cases wherein the marriage is repudiated by the husband. But in India in those days of straightforwardness and honesty, when sales were effected not on stamped paper duly worded, signed, sealed, delivered and registered, but by words of honour uttered from mouth to the ear having only the mother-earth and the space to witness the deed, it was considered essential that such an important ceremony as the marriage between two people should be made known to as many as possible, to minimize the possibility of one of the contracting parties repudiating the marriage *in toto* subsequently. The custom was perhaps designed to achieve this end. By the procession, one and all in the village are appraised of the marriage of the parties and consequently its repudiation at a future date is well nigh impossible in the face of so many witnesses, if one or other party is inclined to do so.

The marriage feast of the Hindus is also proverbial. Every marriage is accompanied by feasts. Almost all the people in the village are invited and fed sumptuously both day and night, and at the end of the meal are given sandal paste, flowers and *pan supari*.

The services of a piper are also requisitioned for the performance during the marriage rites. Music is supposed to scare away the undesirable invisible beings from the marriage *pandals* and the premises.

Now-a-days, phaetons drawn by horses and motor cars

have taken the place of old old palanquins and primitive cars drawn by bullocks, and Washington gas lights the place of oil-fed torches ! The sight of a palanquin with its decorations of tufts of coloured cotton threads going by the names of *Kuñjams*, etc., has now-a-days become very rare indeed ; nor are primitive cars with their decorations with dolls and tinsels shining in the torchlight like sparklers, frequently seen in villages on marriage occasions.

Pyro-technic display during and at the time of the procession has also been resorted to, perhaps to drive away unfavourable influences. From this custom, a proverb also has come into existence which means ' A MARRIAGE WITH ONLY HALF A *Fanam* AND THIS EXPENDITURE INCLUDES THE ITEM OF FIRE-WORKS TOO ! '

As regards the taking in procession round the villages of new *Brahmachāris* and girls that had newly attained puberty, we may say that it is mainly for visiting the various houses and receiving the blessings of the villagers. We may as well call it the return visit.

The giving of milk and fruit to the girl taken in procession may be said to signify the hearty wishes of the inmates of the houses for the prosperity of the girl. It is more or less akin to saying ' May your marriage come to fruition ' or in other words ' May you bring forth children who may have enough nourishment,' fruit in milk denoting perhaps children in the midst of plenty !

MŌTHARAPPAṆAM, I.E., RING-MONEY

DIFFERENT nations and different people have different ways of showing their love and affection for others. Recognition of services and assistance rendered takes different ways, ranging from words of commendation to gifts of costly articles and titles. The Christians show their love to one another during Christmas and New Year days by sending cards containing pithy sayings and expressions of love and good wishes. On marriage occasions and the celebration of birthdays, friends and relations send the bride and bridegroom as well as the individual, whose birthday is being celebrated, marriage presents and birthday gifts. A similar practice is observed by the Hindus also. There is not a Hindu marriage or religious ceremony but is closed with what is called *Āsirvātham* or blessings on the bridal pair or observer of the ceremony. All the people in the village are invited to be present on the occasion to take part in the cumulative blessings on the individuals. Mere acquaintances are given pinches of rice, coloured yellow with turmeric and these they shower on the heads of the recipients of the blessing. But the blessings of friends and relations take tangible material gifts from cash payment to costly ornaments and valuable clothes. Near relatives and intimate friends bring clothes and ornaments, while distant relatives and ordinary friends make presents to the party of a small amount going by the name of *Mōtharappaṇam.* This name was derived perhaps from the use to which the collection was put, namely, in making a ring to decorate the finger with.

During the occasion of the *Āsirvātham* of the Hindu bridal pair, some present gifts to the bride and some to the bridegroom. When *Brahmachāris* newly made are blessed, the blessing also takes the tangible form of gifts of cloth silk or plain, fit to be worn by him. Similarly girls and pregnant women, etc., are given gifts suitable for them and the occasion. The way in which the gifts are presented is striking. The family *Purōhit* or preceptor is given the gifts one by one, and he says aloud, in customary language in vogue, the name of the giver of the gift, his relationship to the recipient and the nature of the object presented. All gifts made are to be recognized by return payment in some special cases, and by gifts of fruits and *pan supari* in other cases.

This custom of return is not found among persons other than the Hindus. It may be intended to serve the purpose of a receipt, acknowledging the receipt of the gift or it may have even deeper significance. Courtesy requires that the recipient should thank the donor and the return gift is perhaps in lieu of the acknowledgment of the gift with thanks. Moreover, the Hindu spirit is such that any favour not returned is considered to be a debt to be repaid sooner or later. If it is not forthwith returned, the donor fears that the favour would remain in his *kārmic* account book as an item to the credit of the donor. In fact many a Hindu on his death-bed sends for his debtor or creditor and closes his accounts with him by paying or receiving a small portion at least of the amount due in full settlement of his claims or otherwise, to avoid coming into future relationship in the next birth to pay or receive payment of this debt. So scrupulous are those with a good conscience !

ĀSIRVĀTHAM, I.E., BLESSING

No nation attaches greater importance to the dictum laid down in the proverb—*Vox Populi, Vox Dei*—which means 'PEOPLE'S VOICE IS THE VOICE OF GOD', than the Hindus. In fact every ceremony observed by the Hindus is to be rounded of and finished with a function called *Āsirvātham.* We may take the most common observance of the Hindus—the annual *Srāddha* to propitiate the *Pitris* or the manes of the departed. There too, after the Brāhmins are sumptuously fed and prior to their departure, they perform a function blessing the performer of the *Srāddha*, and wishing him health, wealth and prosperity. The next common ceremony of the Hindus is the marriage ceremony. Here too, the final function is what is known as *Āsirvātham* or blessing of the bridal pair. The function is considered to be so very important that a kind of cake in the form of a cone going by the name *Āsirvātha Paruppu Thĕngāi* has come to be recognized as an item more or less unavoidable in the programme, even as the Christmas cake is recognized as a *sine qua non* during Christmas feasts.

Even the Hindu *Upanayanam* has its final *Āsirvātham* function in which the newly fledged *Brahmachāri* is bestowed blessings on.

The conduct of the *Āsirvātham* ceremony itself is full of interest. The family priest stands up and is ready to transmit the blessings to the individuals concerned. One by one the friends and relatives of the persons to be bestowed blessings on, stand up with their gifts accompanying their blessings in abstract, to wit, their thoughts of good wishes for the recipients of the gifts and hand them in to the waiting family *guru* or priest. The gift ordinarily consists of gold coins, silver coins, new cloths, ornaments and so on. The *guru* briefly tells the audience assembled who the bestower is, his relationship to the recipient and the nature of the gift itself bestowed, having at first gathered the necessary information and particulars from the giver of the gift. He then hands over the gift with the benedictions to the object of the blessings. This process is repeated till all the gifts brought for the purpose have been duly received by the priest, passed over and acknowledged.

This simple but unique custom is worthy of the spiritually-minded Hindu sages of old, and the passing of the gift and benedictions through the family priest who is in fact considered to be the best friend which the members of the family can have on any occasion, is really the wisest arrangement that can be made to conduct the business in an orderly manner and to bestow the fullest benefit on the person by the cumulative mental force directed towards the audience assembled.

USE OF COW-DUNG

WASHING the floor of the houses with cow-dung is an Indian custom at once unique and interesting to examine its rationale. So far as it is known no nations other than the Hindus follow this custom. The Mahomedans are rather averse to it though of late some of them, convinced of the beneficial effects of the same perhaps, have taken to it. At dawn in the morning, the first work which a lady or her servant maid, if there be one in the house, should do is to sprinkle in front of her house a thick solution of cow-dung after sweeping away the accumulated dirt and rubbish, if any. The part is then decorated with designs formed of rice flour. If this is not done in any of the houses, then one may be sure that some calamity has befallen in that house and some one has perhaps died recently.

This peculiar custom of washing the floor of the whole house with water and cow dung should be observed at least twice in a week, the days of the week considered highly desirable being Tuesdays and Fridays. On all auspicious occasions the floors coated over with water and cow-dung mixed and well stirred are re-mopped with a piece of cloth and covered over with *Kōlam* or designs formed of rice flour. Some use rice flour coloured yellow for the purpose while others make use of a thick solution of fine rice flour obtained by steeping the latter in water. It is also the custom on auspicious occasions like marriage, etc., to have the side of the verandah facing the street covered with broad stripes even about five or six inches in width of white and red colour alternately.

If the floors washed over with cow-dung and water are not re-mopped but allowed to dry without any rice flour decorations covering them, either *Srāddha* or the annual ceremony for the dead is being performed in that house or some one has died a short time ago in that house. The Hindus believe that when water mixed with cow-dung sprinkled or spread over the floors, it removes pollution. In fact the place occupied by a menses woman should be washed with cow-dung and water, as well as the place where the barber exercised his skill on the crown and other parts of a customer in the house of a village Brāhmin, before it becomes free from pollution and fit for frequenting. Further a house from which a corpse is removed to the cremation ground should be washed with cow-dung and watered thoroughly, before it becomes fit for re-occupation of the relatives of the deceased. The mud wall houses in a village are first coated over with a thick layer of cow-dung solution and then whitewashed if necessary.

The above are not the only uses to which cow-dung is put to. Every one knows of the usefulness of dried cakes of cow-dung, as the fuel of the poor people; and of the white ashes obtained by covering thick pieces and balls of dry cow-dung, well kneaded and rendered free from bits of stone, etc., with chaff and setting fire to the heap. The said ashes are considered sacred and the Saivaites or followers of Siva freely smear such ashes over their bodies. The ashes prepared on the *Sivarātri* night are considered highly suited for the purpose and large quantities of these ashes are used in Siva temples not only to pour over the idols to be subsequently distributed among the visitors, but also to burn camphor on before the deity which act is considered to consecrate the ashes very much. Ashes that had undergone the above processes are considered to be highly magnetized or consecrated and people not only smear their foreheads and bodies with them, but also send a fair supply of it to their relatives and friends in other distant places even.

If the deity happens to be a female deity, ashes are not of course made use of, but red saffron powder takes the place and what is said as applicable to the aforesaid holy ashes is applicable to this powder also.

When the plantain or other leaves on which food is served are removed after the meals are over and thrown out, the place or places where those leaves were spread, are washed with cow-dung and water. The Hindus considered saliva as a dangerous medium to spread diseases from one person to another, transferring microbes from one to another. In fact a Hindu Brāhmin would never touch his teeth or tongue with his hands and touch others or other things without first washing his hands immediately in water. Every tyro in physiology knows that through the mouth are thrown out waste matters from the body. If the individual was suffering from contagious diseases, there was every danger of the germs of the diseases spreading through saliva. The cow-dung is considered to possess the germicidal quality and so if the floors are washed over with it the germs are killed. The reason why the floors of house wherefrom corpses are taken out are washed with cow-dung is perhaps due to the reason noted above since people generally die of diseases and diseases are generally caused by germs and consequently a large number of them may be found thrown out from the corpse.

The modes of restoring purity to various inanimate things as prescribed in the *Institutes of Manu* are—

'Of brilliant metals, of gems, and of every thing made with stone, the purification ordained by the wise, is with ashes, water, and earth.

'A golden vessel, not smeared, is cleansed with water only; and every thing produced in water as coral, shells, or pearls, and every stony substance, and a silver vessel not enchased.

'From a junction of water and fire arose gold and silver; and they two, therefore, are best purified by the elements, whence they sprang.

'Vessels of copper, iron, brass, pewter, tin and lead, may be fitly cleansed with ashes, with acids or with water.

'The purification ordained for all sorts of liquids, is by stirring them with *kusa*-grass; for cloths folded, by sprinkling them with hallowed water; for wooden utensils, by planing them.

'For the sacrificial pots to hold clarified butter and juice of the moon-plant, by rubbing them with the hand, and washing them, at the time of the sacrifice.

'Implements to wash the rice, to contain the oblations, to cast them into the fire, to collect, winnow, and prepare the grain, must be purified with water made hot.

'The purification by sprinkling is ordained for grain and cloths in large quantities; but to purify them in small parcels, which a man may easily carry, they must be washed.

'Leathern utensils, and such as are made with cane, must generally be purified in the same manner as cloths; green vegetables, roots, and fruit, in the same manner as with grain.

'Silk and woollen stuff, with saline earths; blankets from Nepal, with pounded arishtas, or *nimba* fruit; vests and long drawers, with the fruit of the *vilva*; mantles of *kshuma*, with white mustard-seeds.

'Utensils made of shells or of horn, of bones or of ivory, must be cleansed by him, who knows the law, as mantles of *kshuma* are purified, with the addition of cows' urine or of water.

'Grass, firewood, and straw, are purified by sprinkling them with water; a house, by rubbing, brushing and smearing with cow-dung; an earthen pot, by a second burning.

But an earthen pot, which has been touched with any spirituous liquor, with urine, with ordure, with spittle, with pus, or with blood, cannot, even by another burning, be rendered pure.

'Land is cleansed by five modes: by sweeping, by smearing with cow-dung, by sprinkling with cows' urine, by scraping, or by letting a cow pass a day and a night on it.

'A thing nibbled by a bird, smelt at by a cow, shaken with a foot, sneezed on, or defiled by lice, is purified by earth scattered over it.

'As long as the scent or moisture, caused by any impurity, remains on the thing soiled, so long must earth and water be repeatedly used in all purifications of things inanimate.'

USE OF TURMERIC

THE use of turmeric (*curcuma longa*) on all auspicious occasions is considered to be highly essential by one and all of the Hindus. Much trade is carried on in dried turmeric root and hundreds of acres are under the cultivation of this root every year. All married women and unmarried girls should use this every day while bathing. Women going to bathe in rivers in villages in Southern India, take with them a bit of this root to prepare a paste of yellow colour to be applied to their faces and legs previous to plunging in the water. Even if they bathe at home they make use of this root. Only widows, who are supposed to be dead to all joys of this world, do not make use of this. On occasions of betrothal, when visiting *Sumaṅgalis* (women with husbands living) and pregnant women, a quantity of this root is taken with betel leaves, areca-nut, red saffron, flowers, fruits, etc., as fitting presents. In fact this article —turmeric root—is so common in all families that a proverb has become current and when a man becomes very poor people say that he is worth not even a *mañjal kombu* (a turmeric root).

The reason for the importance attached to the use of this yellow root is not clear to many. Some say that an application of a paste of this over the skin removes hair and prevents the growth of it. As men would not like their women to be with moustaches and overgrowth of hair on their faces, this paste came to be in use, is the reason given by some. But the real reason seems to be connected with certain beliefs in the denizens of the super-physical world, who are supposed to have connection with the formation and growth of this plant. In fact the Hindus do believe that every form in this world, nay in the solar system itself, is under one or other variety of *dēvas* or super-physical beings.

The yellow colour is said to have power to influence the intellect, since the yellow *dēvas* whose essence is intelligence precipitated this colouring matter in this dense world to form the various yellow substances. Any attempt to be successful should be guided by intellect. Hence has arisen the custom of using turmeric as the most handy yellow substance, not only to symbolize intellect, the guiding factor in the performance of the rituals, but also inducing the flow of influence from the yellow *dēvas* of mental essence.

The reason why ladies make use of this and not men, lies in the fact that they represent power while men are simply the guiding agents of that power.

Fine red colour is said to symbolize love. Mere intellect without love is of no practical use in this world. So it must be tempered with love. This purpose is symbolized and served by the mixture of turmeric and slaked lime used on auspicious occasions as well as by the red saffron largely used by ladies on all auspicious occasions.

Men have not completely given up turmeric. As man and wife are considered to be one in the matter of performance of rituals, and as the wife uses the saffron, there is no necessity for man also to use it. But when he becomes a *Sanyāsin* and renounces the world he uses the yellow robe to denote and symbolize intellect, and red robes love for all created beings.

VAḶAYAL (BANGLE) WEARING

Of the many ornaments worn by the ladies in India *Vaḷayal* and *Kaṅkanam* are perhaps the most common. This ornament is used by one and all, both young and old, the female babies in the cradle included. *Vaḷayal* is glass bangle, while *Kaṅkanam* is a bangle made of lac and covered over with tinsel.

The word *Vaḷayal* is a noun from the verb *vaḷai* which means to surround; and hence *Vaḷayal* may be taken to mean an ornament to surround the wrist.

Kaṅkanam is a word derived from the Sanskrit word *Kaṅgana* a wrist ornament usually worn on the wrist, the tying and untying of the same are important parts of marriage ceremonies. So much importance is attached to the *Kaṅkanam*—a talismanic thread tied round the wrist of brides, bridegrooms and others whose marriage ceremonies are being celebrated that even in cards of invitation sent, this item is given expression to as 'your presence with friends and relations is requested on the occasion of the *Kaṅkana Visarjanam* or the untying and the casting away of the *Kaṅkanam* or the talismanic thread.'

Not only the bangles made of glass and lac are made use of by the womenfolk but also wrist ornaments made of bones, ivory, gold and silver. Though the bangles made of gold, glass and lac are commonly used by almost all women in Southern India, those made of bones, ivory and silver are worn by women of certain communities only. The ancient literatures make mention of the wearing of bangles made of chank as the water used by women wearing this is said to get purified in the process of cooking.

Though in years gone by, glass bangles and lac bangles appear to have been universally worn by women, yet richer classes of people appear to have now given them up in majority of cases and have gone in for bangles and bracelets made of gold or made of gold and set with precious stones. Many kinds of wrist ornaments have since come into use one replacing the other according to the fashion of the day. For example, the wrist ornament that went by the name *Pātli* has almost completely disappeared now.

The use of *Vaḷayal* and *Kaṅkanam* is one of time-worn customs of the Hindus, not only from the point of decoration of the body but also from a religious point of view as will be seen here. A string steeped in turmeric and tied round the wrist with the recital of certain words is said to possess talismanic virtues not only to ward off evil but also to scare away undesirable spirits or elements of the super-physical world.

Much importance was actually attached to the wearing of this *Vaḷayal*. A visit to the shores of the Ganges or other sacred rivers and holy places on the seashore on auspicious occasions will convince even the most sceptic of this fact, since he would find a large number of these *Vaḷayals* thrown by ladies into the waters for the water spirits and the presiding goddesses to wear! Further, when a woman becomes *enceinte* for the first time, during the fifth month or the seventh month after conception, she is decorated with bangles of gold and silver as well as *Vaḷayals* and *Kaṅkanams*. This auspicious ceremony goes by the name of *Vaḷaikāppu* which means protecting wrist ornament or talismanic wrist ornament. Thus it goes without saying that this wearing of the wrist ornaments by ladies during the fifth or the seventh month of her conception was and is being believed by the Hindus to possess virtues sufficient to ward off evil from the evil spirits, etc., hovering about her. It is further said that pregnant women are considered to be more susceptive to the influence of evil spirits than others.

Another explanation may also be offered or we may at least speculate that the custom was intended to bless the woman that she would bring forth many children, each bangle representing a soul symbolically, born as human children, being tied to the circular and even revolving wheel of birth and death. At any rate this unique custom is there ; and a Hindu unless he is a sceptic does follow it even to-day fully believing in its efficacy as it was being done even during the time of his forefathers. Though the rationale has been lost, the long-standing custom is not lost and it is the duty of every true Hindu not to brush such customs aside as silly and useless, but to try to preserve it even though he may not be able to understand the rationale just now. The mental image of a ring formed round an individual or water poured round a person or thing, and light taken round him are said to create barriers preventing evil spirits from approaching near.

The forming by a Brāhmin of a circle with water round his plate of food at the time of eating, as well as the circle formed of water round him when performing his *Sandhyā* and *Mādhyanhikam* the daily offerings of oblations of water to the deities strengthens the explanation given regarding the efficacy of keeping fire, water or even a mental image of a ring round a person or thing. These ring-pass-nots are verily the moats and fortifications surrounding the abode of the soul of a being, making it impossible for the evilly disposed entities to approach the stronghold.

VAGIḌU-PIḶAPPU, I.E., THE PARTING OF THE HAIR

THE Hindu ladies in Southern India wear their hair parted by a furrow on the crown of their head. What is this custom due to ? Ladies in different countries wear their hair arranged in different ways. Some wear it in a single pig-tail while others in two or more pig-tails and so on. A large quantity of curl paper is made use of in the countries in the West to give the hair an artificial curl in place of the one denied by dame nature. But the Hindu ladies wear their hair parted on the crown by a line running from front to back. In the case of grown-up and aged dames, the hair is simply gathered in a knot, whereas young girls and women wear it in a single pig-tail. But every one wears it parted on either side leaving a furrow-like streak of skin exposed on the crown of the head is a time-worn custom.

Like every other Hindu custom this also is followed with a particular significance attached to it. A woman symbolizes *Sakti* or power. There is also a myth emphasizing this statement. Siva, one of the Hindu Trinity, was once conceited and thought that he was the all in all. His wife Umā, wanted to teach him that without her help, he would be able to achieve nothing. With this object in view She, who was always with Him and in Him, left him for a while. Siva all on a sudden felt himself deprived of all his strength and energy to activity ! He was lying in a precarious condition unable even to stir when his wife came there. He prayed to her to lift him up. She told him that he might try to stand up without her help, and as he could not do so he had to acknowledge *her* position as *Sakti* or energy in the world everywhere. There is also another mythical allegory embodied in Hindu *Upanishads* which says that the *Dēvas* (celestials), when they were elated at the success gained over the *Asuras* (demons) thought they had achieved the victory. Umā, that is *Sakti* in the form of a *Yaksha* (a *Dēva* with a body of light), appeared in the court of Indra whose followers *Agni*—the God of fire, *Vāyu*—the God of wind, and others were deprived of their strength by her. Agni was not able to burn even a bit of straw and Vāyu was unable to lift even the lightest of feathers !! Then Indra and others learned the invaluable lesson that without *Sakti* nothing in the universe was possible. This is the reason why *Sakti* is assigned a very important place in every form of worship and in temples. Every *Moorthi* (form of god) has his *Sakti* and without Her He is nothing.

When once this fact is grasped the custom of leaving a furrow on the crown of the woman's head parting the hair into the right half and the left half will become intelligible. It symbolizes the radiation of the positive and the negative energies from a central place.

The Hindu *Yōgis* (sages) say that each thought is a picture formed in the retina of the mind's eye by the temporary completion of the circuit of two electro-magnetic centres in the brain going by the names, pineal gland and the pituitary body, two rudimentary organs in the brain. Just as the two knobs charged with different kinds of electricity when brought near enough, result in the production of a spark, human will brings these organs near enough to flash out a thought-image. This function is always going on in men in the mechanism of their brain, when thoughts flash out in the form of pictures. The furrow-like division of the hair represents only this completion of the circuit resulting in a mental picture. In fact, great philosophers opine that this visible universe and everything it contains is the result of the permanent union of the pineal gland and the pituitary body in the subtle invisible matter in the cosmic brain corresponding to the human brain centres, and this fact is represented and emphasized by the phallic symbol in the Siva temples of the Hindus.

At any rate, the furrow on the crown of a woman's head represents in a masterly manner this completion of the circuit between two mighty positive and negative centres resulting in the mental plane in the formation of the universe in the beginning, to be later on crystallized and materialized into the coarser world we see, need not be lost sight of. It is worthy to be pondered over as the highest philosophical truth symbolically manifested in the simplest possible manner, just in the same way as it is done in many an ordinary custom of the Hindus appearing on its surface to be meaningless.

KŌLAM, I.E., THE FLOUR DECORATION

It is a common thing in Hindu quarters of towns and villages that young maidens in pretty costumes and with cheerful faces are engaged every morning early after sunrise, in forming designs called *Kōlam* in Hindu Tamil phraseology, on the floor in front of each and every one of the houses all along the street, scattering deftly pinches of a white powder; nor is the custom confined to the entrance and approaches only, the interior portions also having their share of the designs. Formed all along the street on either side under the well-trained hands of Hindu maidens, they indeed present a sight at once unique and admirable to a foreigner anxious to learn the manners and customs of the people of the country of his sojourn; nor are they without any interest to one even if he be not a foreigner if he but be aesthetically inclined.

Such artistic designs undoubtedly signify the aesthetic taste of the Hindus. The use of pulverized grain for the purpose has, besides a religious importance has its own moral purpose to serve, to wit, kindness to inferior insects. Again this long standing custom gives the requisite training in free-hand drawing to the young maidens and thus it has also an educative value set upon it.

These floor ornaments formed daily, commonly at the entrance of every Hindu house, contain various devices and they are also connected with the prevalent ideas regarding the evil eye. There is current a Tamil proverb which says, 'If one can hide themselves under a small mat another can conceal himself under the Kōlam' thereby meaning the latter is more cunning.

Some of them are representations of chariots drawn by horses, elephants or bullocks. A few of the designs represent tanks with lotus buds and full-blown and half-blown lotuses floating in their waters. There are also designs representing individual animals like cows, horses, bulls with horns, elephants with tusks and so on. Birds like the peacock, and portions of buildings with steps, ingresses and egresses, are also represented by some of the designs formed.

Many Hindus do not understand the *why* of things; nor do they at all care to understand the same. Hence the valuable customs of ancient Hindus have degenerated, and if at all they exist, they exist only as shells.

Hindu customs generally have particular ends in view, and particular aims to achieve. Moral lessons most of them do teach. Let us try to understand the rationale of this design-forming in front, as well as in the interior of Hindu houses.

Ancient Hindus used rice flour to form the designs and thus fed myriads of ants every day which would otherwise get into undesirable places in the house, and prove very troublesome. Further 'START THE BUSINESS OF A DAY WITH A SACRIFICE' is the Hindu motto. What other better mode of sacrifice could be suggested than this?

But for the degeneration of the custom, powdered limestone would not have taken the place of pulverized corn. Baskets and baskets of powdered limestones, would not be brought to form the designs, if the *why* of things is properly taught. The very object for which the custom was originated, is frustrated by the use of powdered limestone. A very good opportunity for showing mercy and kindness to inferior insects is lost. For every ceremony holy and auspicious, the floor whereon it was to be celebrated was washed clean and filled with designs in rice flour, by the ancient Hindus, who understood the *why* of things. But modern Hindus, who do not care to understand the rationale of things, use powdered limestone in place of pulverized corn or in other words *give stone when bread is asked for.*

Marriage *pandals* (sheds) and places of divine worship used to be decorated with designs, using only rice flour. Nowadays limestone dust takes the place of the rice flour. When a child was born or when a girl attained puberty, the entrance and approaches to the house used to be graced with designs in corn flour. Now behold the people unwittingly scattering powdered limestone on auspicious occasions when food should be scattered everywhere to give expression to the joy they feel! Sugarcandy is distributed to friends on happy occasions and not lumps of stone. Why should not poor insects be fed with rice flour when one's heart is full of joy?

Further bits of stones, which are akin to limestones, are considered inauspicious since they are used only when some one dies, to fix the departed soul in it and to perform the rites for the dead as enjoined in the *Sāstras* of the Hindus. The dictates in *Silpa Sāstras* or the science of architecture are to remove the stones while examining the earth for the selection of house sites and also to avoid the making use of stone pillars in houses intended for dwellings. Certain people would not have even small bits of stone inside a wall or under the ground in the interior of the house and so on because on account of this principle. Such being the case why people use powdered limestone instead of rice flour is a wonder to many who understand the rationale of things.

On inauspicious occasions such as death in a house, various ceremonies are performed and it is not the custom to decorate the floor with designs on those occasions; nor do people observe the custom when annual ceremony called *Sraddha* for the departed manes are performed; but on the contrary people studiously avoid it on those occasions. Hence the design forming in rice flour was intended for auspicious ceremonies only; and so it is that on every marriage and other holy and auspicious occasions we see they are profusely made use of.

Further, that nations differ vastly in their temperaments is a fact admitted everywhere by almost one and all. This is evinced from the literature, art and various other sources of information from different countries and different nations. While one nation or one country is artistically inclined, another country or another nation may have a leaning towards utility more than towards beauty in art, literature and various other things in every day life even. We have heard of people belonging to one nation going to the extant of engaging servants, both male and female, from countries other than their own paying large sums of money as their wages, solely because the servants from their countries are not endowed with particular ideas of taste and decorum. In fact the servants from among their own countrymen and countrywomen, in their opinion, do not possess the satisfactory aesthetic development and ideas of up-to-date fashion in things. There is not a single English novel but has a reference to Parisian fashion in life adopted by refined and up-to-date Englishmen and women as well as by men and women of other countries also. Taking an article from France and comparing it with one from England, in the former we are sure to find an attention to beauty in the shape of carving, etc., while the latter almost always remains quite plain though durable and useful.

The people of India of old were fond of beauty and this can be seen even by comparing modern bronze lamps and brass plates going by the names *Kuthuviḷakku* and *Tāmbāḷam* with similar articles manufactured in olden days, say a quarter of a century before, not to speak of many other articles. The silk and lace borders of cloths from Indian looms and the several kinds of cloths of pure silk and those of silk and cotton thread mixed, stand unrivalled for beauty of design and art even to-day though the contact with the ruling nation has almost killed in the nation all feelings of pride in their ancient artistic temperament. The ancient Hindu Rājas had an eye both to beauty as well as use in everything they did. They had planted on both sides of roads banyan trees and they had dug many tanks at short intervals over which bloomed lotus flowers and water lilies delighting the eyes of the weary travellers. The famous Queen Maṅgammāḷ while she was administering the Madura country, had banyan trees planted on the sides of the trunk road leading to Dindigul from Madura. But nowadays we find the banyan trees replaced by tamarind trees to afford income to the Taluk Boards for the maintenance of roads and tanks decorated not with the beautiful aquatic flowers but water weeds of ugly appearance to enable greater breeding facilities for fish—another source of income to Government! Thus we see that the once artistic Indian nation has now become highly inartistic. Their brass plates and bronze lamp-stands do not show artistic designs as they used to do in bygone days. They have imbibed from the civilization of their ruling race the tendency to look to profit and not to the cultivation of the sense of creating and appreciating beauty in everything. The temple towers and temple cars afford in the innumerable images, flowers, etc., formed and carved in them, sufficient evidence in support of this statement.

Everything relating to the household management rests with the women and not with the men. The cooking of the daily meal, the scrubbing and clearing arrangements of the kitchen utensils, *pūja sāmāns* and the floors, are always considered to be the daily routine work of women and not men. Even a beggar when begging says 'Madam! give me alms!' and not 'Sir! give me alms!' Further, the wife is called in Sanskrit *Grihiṇi* which means the manager of the household duties. Every woman in India is expected to rise from her bed with the cock's crow and the first and foremost duty she has to do is to sweep the house entrance clean, sprinkle water to keep down the dust and decorate the place with *Kōlam* or artistic designs using pulverized rice. Having performed this, she goes inside the house and after having cleaned and washed the floors there with fresh cow's dung mixed with water, decorates them with *Kōlam* or designs formed of rice flour. This custom is being followed nowadays in very few houses satisfactorily in the way in which it has to be done. Several innovations have crept in simply because the rationale and basic principles of the custom have been lost sight of even as it has been the case in several other ancient things. Suppose the temple cars are not drawn by men but are propelled by steam or electricity, would it give any delight to the people, we wonder? Suppose men do not use the mouth and the tongue and the teeth but simply manage to put their food into the stomach by some miraculous and ingenious means, would it give as much pleasure as it gives people now, we also wonder!! Of course people go on pilgrimage to distant holy places by express trains and we do wonder whether it gives to people as much pleasure and benefit as it was giving to people of bygone days who took months of tiresome journey to fulfil their vow. Only a hungry man can appreciate what the satisfaction of hunger means. Only people who do not own motor cars and carriages drawn by horses, can understand and appreciate the bliss of rest after a tiresome walk. Similarly, even in following this simple, beautiful and unique custom of 'floor decoration' our women need the cunning of their hands. But tinkers have stencils for designs ready for a few annas and alas! our ladies nowadays finish their *Kōlam* business in a few seconds while those in ancient days had to spend hours in this interesting occupation! Even as the gramophone has deprived the people to some extent at least of the real pleasure of hearing songs, etc., from the first-hand source, even as cinemas have almost thrown into the background our theatres and even as the capacity of people to enact scenes mentally after reading books is threatened at least to some extent by them, this system of floor decoration also followed just now has lost its primitive aim and pleasure derived from it.

Is it not desirable to revive and restore the ancient system of this unique custom and know also the rationale of it, the original aim, the 'how' and the 'why' of the thing which our women are following from time immemorial?

NĀGA-PRATISHṬA, I.E., INSTALLATION OF SNAKE IMAGES

THERE is a peculiar custom among the Hindus going by the name *Nāga-Pratishṭa*. It consists in the establishment of *Nāga* (snake) images made out of stone under the spreading branches of the village *Asvatta* (*ficus religiosa*) tree on the banks of the village tank or river flowing by, with the enjoined religious rites and ceremonies. Generally barren women observe this custom of *Nāga-Pratishṭa* and circumambulate the sacred *Asvatta* tree to shake off their sterile curse and be blessed with offsprings. Strange to see that people who observe this custom are, at least in many of the cases, successful in getting their wishes gratified ; else this custom could not have withstood the onslaught of the materialistic waves of centuries !

Women of flabby constitution are in most cases liable to be barren. Indian women as a rule do not have the benefit of outdoor exercises except when they go round on annual tours of pilgrimage. So some sort of exercise is of absolute necessity for them to shake off their barrenness. Women belonging to the working classes are, generally, in most cases have many children born to them whereas those belonging to the richer classes are barren and if at all they bring forth issues, they are few and not overstrong as the children of the working classes are.

The wise preceptors of the rich people in bygone days wanted to give the rich ladies some sort of exercise coupled with a mental attitude favourable for child-bearing. Religious belief was pressed into service. As the ancient Āryans worshipped nature by worshipping certain animals having special characteristics of the elements they desired to worship and as the serpent happened to symbolize wisdom and the one commonly considered sacred and hence greatly venerated, it was selected as the fittest object to inspire veneration in women. As the living serpent was not a safe object to be kept near, stone image of one took its place. Scientists tell us that the mental attitude is an essential thing for a woman to conceive and give birth to a healthy child. The serpent, symbolical of the highest form of wisdom, should create a wise mental attitude in the mind of the woman to give birth to a worthy issue.

The reason why it was located under a tree and that too the sacred *Asvatta* tree lies in the fact that it is a tree, royal in appearance to inspire veneration in human beings and further it affords a pleasant shade because of its spreading foliage on the cool banks of the village tank or river. From a medical point of view, the Hindu physicians considered the sacred tree *Asvatta* to possess miraculous virtues and medicinal properties, and consequently if any male or female remained in its vicinity he or she would surely be the better for it.

The reason why the image was not placed inside the house and worshipped is mainly because of the fear that 'FAMILIARITY MAY BREED CONTEMPT.' The second reason is that the open air on the banks of tanks and rivers is more favourable to recoup health and vitality whereas the confined atmosphere of a house would only make them more sickly if they took exercise of the nature intended by the then wise that they should take.

The reason why barren ladies generally throw off their barrenness and become *enceinte* is that they take a good exercise in the exhilarating early hours of the morning, dwelling upon the one thought that she should conceive and bring forth a child. These are *the* things necessary, namely, a healthy body which is furnished by the circumambulation of the *Nāga* image or images under the sacred tree, and a mind congenial and favourable to become *enceinte.* After all perhaps there is no miracle performed here but only favourable conditions for nature to effect its purpose, created.

SATI, I.E., CREMATION ALIVE

ONE of the most important and widely followed Indian customs, now *not at all* followed, is the custom in which the wife becomes the *Satī* of her lord. If a woman lost her husband she would also put an end to her existence by ascending the funeral pyre. This custom went by the name of *Saha-gamanam* or 'going with her lord.' Different explanations are offered for the origin of this seemingly peculiar and inhuman custom is that foreign invaders like the Muhammadans carried away the widows and subjected them to unheard of cruelty. Life without a husband to protect her was considered to be worse than death during those unsettled days. Hence probably the widows in certain cases voluntarily became the *Sati* to escape from the inevitable dishonour at the hands of the beastly foreign invaders. In other cases she was forced to become as *Satī* by her relations who held views similar to that noted above.

When Lord William Bentinck (A.D. 1828–35) assisted by Rāja Rām Mōhan Rōy, desired to put an end to this evil custom in Bengal he was surely influenced by a feeling of pity for the poor miserable widows who to gain the good opinion of the people that she was a *Pati-vrathai* or faithful wife of her devoted husband—first entered the pyre but subsequently tried hard to escape from the hands of the people who forcibly held her down till she was burnt to death. But can we for a moment say that the relatives of the woman becoming a *Satī* had no feelings of pity ? Assuredly her parents, brothers and sisters, even when the custom first originated, ought to have rebelled against the inhuman custom forced on them by social tyranny. But we have no evidence that anything of the kind was *ever* done and consequently we must take it that the woman who was to become a *Satī* was able to do so serenely and without pains and her relatives originally were quite certain that her lot was not as horrible as the people of the time of Lord William Bentinck took it to be. So it may be interesting to know why many in those days were in favour of *Satī*. The bed-rock of Hindu religious faith and belief is that *one can never cease to exist*. His body may be burnt to ashes but he should have a sort of conscious existence somewhere always and in this conscious existence he is capable of enjoying the company of others in a similar state of existence even as one human being here is able to enjoy the company of others. Hence the wife who becomes a *Satī* has an unbroken enjoyment of the company and help of her husband in the other world.

Regarding the agony the *Satī* had to undergo on the funeral pyre. They say that the Brāhmin priests of bygone days knew of a plant, the juice of which when mixed with sandal-paste and rubbed freely over the body of the would-be *Satī* made her insensible to heat. So when her body was being consumed by the fire she felt no pain or even unpleasant sensations. As we are seeing daily people undergoing operations under chloroform without even the slightest knowledge of it, it is not surprising that the virtues of certain plants were known to a select few of those days and the knowledge perished perhaps with those persons; even now the injection of some drugs makes certain required parts of the body sensationless for the doctor to operate upon and hence it is quite possible that there may be plants of the kind referred to above with special properties. Have we not got the drugs opium and ganja both strong intoxicants? They say that there was even a plant or creeper called *Sōmalata* the juice of which was a greater intoxicant than many other similar drugs, and the ancient Hindus drank a kind of preparation from it called *Sōmapāna* which they said freed them from all sins.

The *Institutes of Manu* on the laws concerning women mentions :—

'By a girl, or by a young woman, or by a woman advanced in years, nothing must be done, even in her own dwelling place, according to her mere pleasure.

'In childhood must a female be dependent on her father; in youth, on her husband; her lord being dead, on her sons; if she have no sons, on the near kinsmen of her husband; if he left no kinsmen, on those of her father; if she have no paternal kinsmen, on the sovereign: a woman must never seek independence.

Never let her wish to separate herself from her father, her husband, or her sons; for, by a separation from them, she exposes both families to contempt.'

SAKUNAM OR OMEN

OF the many unique customs prevalent among the Hindus, *Sakunam* or Omen is perhaps one of the most interesting and worthy of notice. Certain days of the week are considered inauspicious for journeys in certain directions, to wit, Mondays and Saturdays are inauspicious for a journey towards the East; while Tuesdays and Wednesdays are inauspicious for a journey towards the North; Fridays and Sundays are considered quite unsuited to start on a journey towards the West, while Thursdays are regarded as undesirable days for undertaking journeys to places in the South.

The cries of certain birds and animals are said to forebode success or failure or even death when heard at the time of discussing a subject or at the beginning of an undertaking. To quote an example the braying of an ass or a donkey is generally considered to be good; while the chirping of a lizard is auspicious or inauspicious in accordance with the particular directions on particular days of the week. The hooting of the owl is auspicious or inauspicious according to the number of times the hooting is repeated by the bird.

Certain asterisms are suitable for certain specific purposes while the same will be considered highly inauspicious for certain other purposes. Certain months of the Hindu year are considered highly inauspicious for marriages and occupation of houses, especially houses newly built; while some months are said to be highly auspicious for the performance of all auspicious ceremonies.

The arrival of guests is believed to be foretold by the cawing of a crow in a house while the wailing of a dog in the street or the village is considered to forebode death.

All the above statements do not come strictly under Omens, which embrace only the sneezing of a man or a woman and the cry of certain birds and animals and the arrival of certain persons and objects in front and the passing across the path of certain birds and animals.

The sight of certain animals is said to be auspicious while their cries are inauspicious ; while, it is considered desirable to hear the cries of and not to see certain animals. A jackal, for example, can only be seen and not heard while a donkey can only be heard and not seen. Both the sight and the cry are auspicious in the case of certain creatures like the Brāhmani-Kite, while both of them are inauspicious if it happened to be the vulture or some such bird.

The passage of certain birds and animals from right to left or from left to right of an individual on his way forebodes good or evil to him or his undertaking, according to the kind of animal or bird crossing the path.

A maiden, a cow, fruits, flowers, curd, animals like elephants, bulls and horses, Brāhmins, grains, gold, sandal-paste, lotus flowers, fried rice, cooked rice, corpses, pearls, a cow with its calf and a mother with her child and certain other things are considered to be desirable and auspicious objects to meet on the way by an individual or individuals proceeding on a journey and the hearing of the sounds of music is also considered to be highly auspicious on all occasions.

Meeting on the way a deformed man or a man with dishevelled or matted hair or with his head anointed with oil, red flowers, wet-cloth, a potter, a pig, a snake, a hare or salt ; or hearing on the way weeping or lamentations are considered highly inauspicious omens that might jeopardize even the life of the person proceeding on the journey, not to speak of the certainty of failing in the object with which the journey was perhaps undertaken. Birds like crows, parrots, peacocks, etc., and Brāhmani-kite and animals like jackal, tiger and buffalo may cross the path from left to right and it forebodes good. But if they crossed from right to left the same forebodes evil and woe to the person undertaking the journey or failure of the undertaking itself. Animals like cats, snakes and hares, if they cross the path at all, are said to forebode evil and disaster. Meeting a single Brāhmin, two Sūdras, three Vaisyas, four Kshatriyas, two new pots, widow or widows and the hearing of the grunt of pigs are also considered to be inauspicious ; whereas two Brāhmins, one Sūdra and a woman having her husband alive are considered to forebode good if they happen to come before the man or woman proceeding on the journey. If the light goes out when a question relating to important subjects is being discussed, it forebodes evil and if there is a drizzle when about to go on journey, it also forebodes evil.

An individual believing in the omens would *never* proceed on his journey, however urgent his business might be, if the omens were not satisfactory. There have been many pre-arranged marriages stopped on account of the unsatisfactory nature of the omen.

We may try to understand the rationale for this time-worn belief. 'Faith' and 'Belief' are two fundamental expressions of the Hindu religious ideals that have given rise to pithy sayings and humorous anecdotes. 'CHILDREN AND GOD RESORT TO PERSONS AND PLACES WHERE THEY ARE MADE MUCH OF' is a household saying ; and this is significant as emphasizing the above statement. Further the following anecdote also illustrates the above facts :—In a small village there was a poor farmer and he had a scythe made as an offering to *Ayyanār*—the village guardian deity, to fulfil a certain vow of his, and having placed it in front of the deity in the temple he returned home to take his meals.

Meanwhile a thief, who was an unbeliever in God, passed that way. Seeing the nice new scythe, he took possession of it and was going on his way. The deity in a rage is said to have hastened to the farmer, slapped him on the face and told him to hasten after the thief to recover his scythe ! ! !

When once the ' Faith ' and the ' Belief ' are conceded among the masses of the Hindus the rationale regarding omen must appear clear. They believe in omens and their belief is justified by the results.

By way of some scientific explanation it might be said that all animals, plants and minerals are under the influence of one planet or another and the intelligences controlling and guiding them are called *Dēvatas* (celestials). So it goes without saying that everything in this world is being guided by one or other of those intelligences working together for common good. Human beings by their belief and faith draw the attention of those intelligences and they show them by bringing about or utilizing chances of men and animals going from one place to another to indicate what is going to happen. These creatures cannot prevent or modify what is going to happen in the least, but they merely show unwittingly that the business will be delayed or the object will be frustrated.

Anyhow the fact remains that the omens prove true at least in the majority of cases and consequently do not deserve to be brushed aside as superstition as some are inclined to do ; but deserve to be scrutinized and studied.

No custom would continue to be observed or followed unless it is found to be efficacious in certain things or useful and this custom of observing *Sakunam* or 'omen' has stood for ages. Further the majority of the Hindus know that there is something inexplicable in this custom which by its truth fills them with wonder by the wonderful results both good, bad and indifferent according to the nature of the omens themselves.

PAÑCHA-PAKSHI SĀSTRAM OR THE SCIENCE OF THE FIVE BIRDS

AMONG the many unique scientific treatises of the Hindus there is one going by the name of *Pañcha-Pakshi Sāstram*, forming a portion of the Hindu astronomical science. Twenty-seven forms of constellations are recognized by the Hindu astrologers in the moon's path. Each is called a lunar mansion and in each of which the moon happens to be each day. These lunar mansions are considered by the astrologers to be of great practical consequence from their good or evil influence not only at the time of birth of an individual but also during his lifetime. The situation of the moon in this or that *Nakshatram* at the moment is considered to regulate the occurring of an event affecting the individual concerned. Every person is born with his special star, mansion or *Nakshatram*, by whatever name we may call it, in which the moon was at the moment of his or her birth. The *Nakshatrams*, are a source of infinite terror to the Hindus of all castes. They are consulted at births and marriages and in all times of difficulty, sickness and so on. Days and events become lucky or unlucky according to the decision of these mansions.

It is not possible to say when these twenty-seven stars which are in the moon's path were created. But they are *Kalpam* after *Kalpam* (several great ages) along with other objects of creation destroyed, recreated, maintained for the next *Kalpam*, and again destroyed. The objects of creation are not quite the same at the beginning of each *Kalpam*, because the good and bad actions outstanding against each object of creation at the end of the preceding *Kalpam* differ ; but in the case of the permanent *dēvatas* (celestials) who do not return to the earth after their stay in *Swarga* (heaven) as the result of the good deeds is over, the fresh creation is quite the same at the beginning of each *Kalpam*. Every constellation, whether it is a fixed star or a planet, is a spherical body and it has a deity which looks after it. The spherical body or *Maṇḍalam* as it is called, is inanimate ; while the deity which has charge of it has a soul and is subject to the orders of the supreme deity, as well as to the orders of the minor deity, under whose command they are placed. All the spherical bodies including the earth. attract each other, and move in harmony in perfect accordance with the rules laid down by the supreme deity in Vēdas and in astrology. Every sphere attracts every other sphere and attracts also every living object in every other sphere. It is this attraction that constitutes the influence which the fixed stars and planets exercise over the living objects on the earth, and the nature of each influence is described in astrology. Astrology is part of Vēdas and every person who has faith in the Vēdas must place faith in astrology. The Vēdas are intended to reveal truths, which human reason cannot discover, and which must therefore be accepted without questioning. No cross-examination should be directed against those truths. Implicit faith must be placed on Vēdic revelations.

Every function, which every living being on earth performs, is the work of some one or more of these deities. The deities work every living being according to the *Karma* (action in the previous birth) which are outstanding against it. God works every living being through the agency of these deities. Every thought which arises in the mind, every emotion which arises in the heart, and every act which the various limbs of every living body perform, is the work of one or more of these deities. In the absence of these deities, there would be no work in the world. Again in the absence of the sun, moon, planets and stars there will be no means of measuring time.

These *Nakshatrams* or lunar mansions are grouped under 'five birds,' namely: 1. The HAWK, 2. The OWL, 3. The CROW, 4. The COCK and 5. The PEACOCK. Hence each individual has not only his own *Nakshatram* but also his own bird out of these five. These birds are said to be in any one of the five states, namely: 1. EATING, 2. WALKING, 3. RULING, 4. SLEEPING and 5. DYING during the five watches or divisions of twelve hours of both the night and day time of each day of the week. Further, these states vary in the dark fortnight from what they were during the week days of the bright fortnight.

The time most auspicious for going on a voyage or a journey, for commencing agricultural operations, for advancing against enemies, for going to ask favours of persons in power, for purchases and sales and so on are when his or her bird is either eating or ruling. The next best time is when the bird is walking which state is not very good either. The hour in which his or her bird is either asleep or dying is the worst hour that could be selected for any good attempt and is generally considered to be the most inauspicious for any undertaking.

The arrangement of the state of the birds in the order of importance is: 1. Ruling, 2. Eating, 3. Walking, 4. Sleeping and 5. Dying. Eating state is considered to be three-fourth important while walking has only half of the importance of the eating state. Sleeping state is considered to be half as important as walking state, while the dying bird is half of the sleeping one.

The table furnishing the bird under which, he or she is

placed from the *Nakshatram* or lunar mansion in which he or she was born is given in all the *Pañchāṅgam* of Indian calendar; so named as it is comprised of five limbs, namely: 1. the *Tithi*, 2. the *Vāram*, 3. the *Nakshatram*, 4. the *Yōgam* and 5. the *Karaṇam*. A man desiring prosperity pays attention to the *Tithi*. One desirous of long life understands everything about *Vāram* or the days of the week. The *Nakshatrams* are resorted to for being freed from sins. The *Yōgam* is intended for obtaining immunity from diseases. The *Karaṇam* is said to secure for the observer success in all undertakings. Hence it was that the recital of the *Pañchāṅgam* was in vogue in olden days in all palaces and in temples in the presence of the central deity as soon as the day opened as the first item in order that the actions of the day may close happily. According to the '*Inscriptions of the Madras Presidency*' on the west and south walls of the *Maṇḍapa* in front of the central shrine in the Visvanātha-swāmi temple at Tenkāsi in the district of Tinnevelly there is a record of the Pāṇḍya King Sunbaka-Sundara-Pāndyadēva *alias* Vīra-Pāndyadēva, dated Saka 1384 (A.D. 1462) registering the gift of houses and shares in the village of Vīra-Pāṇḍya-Chadurvēdimaṅgalam to twenty-four Brāhmanas for reading the *Pañchāṅga*. (Indian calendar), etc.

Nakshathras	Sign used in native Astronomy	Approximately corresponding European Constellation
	THE HAWK	
Asvini	Horse's head ...	Part of Arietis (Hamel).
Bharani	Yoni, triangle or fire-place.	Musca (Hamel).
Kārthikai ...	Razor	Pleiades (Sowr).
Rōhini	Cart	Hyades (Sowr).
Mirukasīrisham ...	Antelope's head ...	Head of Orion (Jabbaur).
	THE OWL	
Thiruvādirai ...	Gem, Coral, or burning coal.	Part of Orion (Jabbaur).
Punarpūsam ...	House, bow or large sea-boat.	Part of Gemini (Jowzah).
Pūsam	Arrow, string or looking glass with handle.	Part of Cancer (Sartaun).
Āyilyam ...	Potter's wheel, Serpent or sloping stone Palanquin.	Do.
Magam ...	House, or yoke.	Part of Leo (Asad).
Pūram	Conch, two small squares or legs of bedstead.	Do.
	THE CROW	
Uttiram ...	Bed, two small squares, or legs of bedstead.	Part of Leo (Asad).
Hastham ...	Hand	Part of Corvus (Ghooraub).
Chithrai	Pearl	Part of Virgo (Soomboola).
Svāti	Coral bead, ruby or small bringal.	Part of Bootes (Awwah).
Visākam ...	Circle, gateway or arch.	Part of Lib (Meezaun) and Scorpio (Akrab).
......	......	......

Nakshathras	Sign used in native Astronomy	Approximately corresponding European Constellation
	THE COCK	
Anusham ...	Row of oblations, umbrella in hand, or bow.	Part of Scorpio (Akrab).
Kēttai	Ring, umbrella in hand, or spear.	Do.
Mūlam ...	Lion's tail, leaping lion, or trumpet.	Do.
Poorādam ...	Elephant's tooth, two double squares, or legs of bedstead.	Part of Sagittarius (Kows).
Uttirādam ...	Do. ...	Do.
	THE PEACOCK	
Tiruvōnam ...	Triangle or three footsteps.	Part of Aquila (Ookaub).
Avittam ...	Drum	Part of Dolphin (Doolfeen).
Sadayam ...	Circle	100 stars of Aquarius (Dalo).
Poorattādi ..	Couch, double head figure, two double squares, or legs of Rāvana's bedstead.	Part of Pegasus (Faras ool Azam).
Uthirattādi ...	Do. ...	Part of Andromedae (Mirat i Moosal Silah) and Pegasus (Faras ool Azam).
Rēvati ...	Tabor, or fish ...	32 stars in Pisces (Hoot).

Names of days in the week	Names of birds	BRIGHT — DAY TIME — First watch	Second watch	Third watch	Fourth watch	Fifth watch
Sunday and Tuesday.	Hawk ...	E	W	R	S	D
	Owl ...	W	R	S	D	E
	Crow ...	R	S	D	E	W
	Cock ...	S	D	E	W	R
	Peacock ...	D	E	W	R	S
Monday and Wednesday.	Hawk ...	D	E	W	R	S
	Owl ...	E	W	R	S	D
	Crow ...	W	R	S	D	E
	Cock ...	R	S	D	E	W
	Peacock ...	S	D	E	W	R
Thursday ...	Hawk ...	S	D	E	W	R
	Owl ...	D	E	W	R	S
	Crow ...	E	W	R	S	D
	Cock ...	W	R	S	D	E
	Peacock ...	R	S	D	E	W
Friday ...	Hawk ...	R	S	D	E	W
	Owl ...	S	D	E	W	R
	Crow ...	D	E	W	R	S
	Cock ...	E	W	R	S	D
	Peacock ...	W	R	S	D	E
Saturday ...	Hawk ...	W	R	S	D	E
	Owl ...	R	S	D	E	W
	Crow ...	S	D	E	W	R
	Cock ...	D	E	W	R	S
	Peacock ...	E	W	R	S	D

R = Ruling.
E = Eating.
W = Walking.
S = Sleeping.
D = Dying.

FORTNIGHT

NIGHT TIME

First watch	Second watch	Third watch	Fourth watch	Fifth watch
D R E S W	W D R E S	S W D R E	E S W D R	R E S W D
W D R E S	S W D R E	E S W D R	R E S W D	D R E S W
S W D R E	E S W D R	R E S W D	D R E S W	W D R E S
E S W D R	R E S W D	D R E S W	W D R E S	S W D R E
R E S W D	D R E S W	W D R E S	S W D R E	R E S W D

R = Ruling.
E = Eating.
W = Walking.
S = Sleeping.
D = Dying.

Names of days in the week	Names of birds	DARK DAY TIME First watch	Second watch	Third watch	Fourth watch	Fifth watch
Sunday and Tuesday.	Cock ...	E	D	S	R	W
	Hawk ...	W	E	D	S	R
	Owl ...	D	S	R	W	E
	Peacock ...	S	R	W	E	D
	Crow ...	R	W	E	D	S
Monday and Saturday.	Cock ...	R	W	E	D	S
	Hawk ...	S	R	W	E	D
	Owl ...	W	E	D	S	R
	Peacock ...	E	D	S	R	W
	Crow ...	D	S	R	W	E
Wednesday ...	Cock ...	S	R	W	E	D
	Hawk ...	D	S	R	W	E
	Owl ...	R	W	E	D	S
	Peacock ...	W	E	D	S	R
	Crow ...	E	D	S	R	W
Thursday ...	Cock ...	W	E	D	S	R
	Hawk ...	R	W	E	D	S
	Owl ...	E	D	S	R	W
	Peacock ...	D	S	R	W	E
	Crow ...	S	R	W	E	D
Friday ...	Cock ...	D	S	R	W	E
	Hawk ...	E	D	S	R	W
	Owl ...	S	R	W	E	D
	Peacock ...	R	W	E	D	S
	Crow ...	W	E	D	S	R

R = Ruling.
E = Eating.
W = Walking.
S = Sleeping.
D = Dying.

FORTNIGHT

NIGHT TIME

First watch	Second watch	Third watch	Fourth watch	Fifth watch
W E R S D	D S E W R	R W S D E	E D W R S	S R D E W
E D W R S	S R D E W	W E R S D	D S E W R	R W S D E
D S E W R	R W S D E	E D W R S	S R D E W	W E R S D
R W S D E	E D W R S	S R D E W	W E R S D	D S E W R
S R D E W	W E R S D	D S E W R	R W S D E	E D W R S

R = Ruling.
E = Eating.
W = Walking.
S = Sleeping.
D = Dying

LIZARD CHIRPING

THE Hindus have belief in several things of which the chirping of the lizard and the hooting of the owl are two of them. These two creatures are supposed to foretell by their chirping and hooting what is going to befall to certain individuals in certain houses. So firm-rooted and strong has been this belief among the people from time immemorial that there are separate books on lizard chirping and owl's hooting. Not only the chirping but also the falling of a lizard on particular portions of the body of a man portends good or evil to him.

If a lizard happens to fall on the head of an individual, then he should be prepared for some rebellion from or caused by others disturbing his peace of mind. If the creature happens to drop on the tuft of hair, it foretells some gain to the person concerned. If it falls on the head, then it indicates death. He who may have the good fortune to receive a falling lizard on his forehead, may expect coronation and if it drops on the face, he may have the opportunity of seeing some relatives soon. Falling on the eye-brows, the lizard prophesizes royal favour and its fall on the upper lip indicates loss of wealth and fall on the nether lip, gain of wealth. The fall of the lizard on other portions of the body indicates good or evil as follows :—

On the nose its fall forebodes sickness and disease ; on the right ear, long life ; on the left ear, gain in trade ; on the eyes, imprisonment ; on the chin, royal punishment ; on the mouth, some source of fear ; on the neck, destruction of enemies ; on the right arm, general health ; on the left arm, sexual enjoyment ; on the right wrist, trouble of one kind or other ; on the navel, gain of precious stones ; on the two sides, immense gain ; on the thighs, unhappiness to parents ; on the knees and ankles, general good ; on the feet, impending travel ; on the buttocks, general good ; on the nails, loss of wealth ; on the penis, penury and want ; on the left hand, sorrow ; on the right hand, misery ; on the back, destruction ; on the anus, gain of money ; on the toes of the feet, fear ; on the left hand fingers, sorrow ; on the right hand fingers, fear from royal displeasure and so on.

As regards the chirping of the lizard and what it portends it is said that the direction from which the chirping is heard on particular days of the week have to be taken into consideration. The following table has been arranged to indicate what the chirping portends on particular days in particular directions :—

On Sundays, the chirping foretells fear, if from the east ; evil, if from the south-east ; good, if from the south ; opportunity to see relatives, if from south-west ; quarrel, if from west ; gain of new cloth, if from north-west ; gain of gems, if from north ; general gain, if from north-east ; success, if from above and failure in attempts, if from the ground below.

On Mondays, the chirping is said to prophesy as noted below :—

East, gain of wealth ; south-east, rebellion ; south, enmity ; south-west, quarrel ; west, reception from king ; north-west, calamity ; north, gain of new cloth ; north-east, marriage ; sky, evil and floor, prosperity.

On Tuesdays, the good or evil indicated by the chirping is as noted below :—

East, prosperity ; south-east, gain of relatives ; south, sorrow ; south-west, enmity ; west, success ; north-west, news from distant parts ; north, fear from enemies ; north-east, gain of vehicles ; sky, journeys and ground, great gain.

On Wednesdays, the chirping denotes joy, if from east; gain of wealth, if from south-east; bodily sickness, if from south; loss of relatives, if from south-west; fear, if from west; loss of wealth, if from north-west; happiness, if from north; want of success, if from north-east; good news, if from above and prosperity, if from below.

On Thursdays, the good or evil indicated is as follows:—

Calamity, if the chirping is from the east; good reception from relatives, if from south-east; gain of wealth, if from south; success in all the undertakings, if from south-west; loss, if from west; good news, if from north-west; failure, if from north; good meals, if from north-east; rebellion, if from above or from below.

On Fridays, good news, if from east; decoration, if from south-east; visit of relatives, if from south; good news, if from south-west; joy, if from west; quarrel and rebellion in the house, if from north-west; quarrelsome and rebellious words, if from north; victory over the enemy, if from north-east; gain of things, if from above and freedom from pollution, if from below.

On Saturdays, good words if from east; gain of wealth and sandal paste, if from south-east; audience with the king, if from south; sickness, if from south-west; gain of new cloth, if from west; relationship with a new woman, if from south-west; pleasing or agreeable news, if from north; fear from thieves, if from north-east; failure in attempts, if from above and success in everything, if from below.

As regards the hooting of the night-bird the owl, people say that if it hoots once, it indicates death; if it hoots twice, it foretells success; if thrice, relationship with women is indicated; if four times, rebellion; if five times, travel; if six times, the arrival of some dependants; if seven times, loss of things; if eight times, sudden death; if nine or ten times, general good.

Sneezing also is good or bad according to the number of times sneezed. Sneezing once shows failure, but sneezing twice is considered to be a good omen.

The particulars furnished above should not be taken to mean literally. They may be supposed to indicate good or bad generally. If it is stated that gems would be gained, actual gems need not be gained. It may be an exaggerated way of telling that good might result. The son of a poor man born in an auspicious hour entitling him to be a king need not become a king. He may be given the king's part in a drama! So the good or evil results should be prophesied after considering the persons, time and place.

RĒKA SĀSTRAM, I.E., PALMISTRY

THE science of Palmistry has been in existence not only in this land of ours, namely, India, but also in other countries as well. It is a science which deals with the formation of the hands and their digits, the classification of the knowledge respecting these and the prophecy or fate as revealed by the hands and their lines. Though some are inclined to treat this subject with contempt, there are others who sincerely hold that within fairly broad lines a clear indication can be given of the general fate and fortune of the individual who submits his palms to one versed in this subject. Palmistry is not the discovery and practice of yesterday, but is a science thousands of years old. An individual with a fine textured hand would be refined in nature. It should be borne in mind that the significations drawn from other indications from other sources may be modified by this. A very smooth fine texture of the skin would annul evidences contradictory to what has been set forth above. A rough coarse texture would emphasize indications of insensitiveness to the finer qualities of life. Flexibility of the hands and fingers indicate refined capacities in the mind. A suppleness in the joints shows mental activity that enables the individual to take broader view of things. He could see both sides of a question or situation and hence would not be stubborn in his views, but would be ready to modify his views, etc., easily. If the joints, hands and fingers be not flexible we may safely assert that the mind of the person is rigid and unbending and that it has decided upon its course which it neither desires nor intends to forsake even if fresh evidence to the contrary be forthcoming. Elasticity of the hand generally indicates the person to be trustworthy and able, whereas the owner of a hand that is flabby and immobile may be safely described as one of idle temperament without the desire for strenuous life. Further he would be inconsistent, and deceptive for the reason that he lacks individuality and character. The shape of the hands as a whole and the shape of the fingers, afford sufficient indications about the temperament, etc., of the individual. A long hand usually indicates capacity for detail and mental strength, whereas a broad hand shows dashing qualifications in the individual combined with physical strength. As regards shape, fingers may be described as pointed, conic, spatulate or square. As regards character they may be classed under heads long, short, smooth or knotted.

Persons with pointed finger tips are generally of artistic temperament lacking sometimes in the ability to do great things themselves. Men with conic fingers are impulsive, sensitive, prone to exaggeration, restless, volatile and pessimistic and optimistic by turns. Spatulate finger tips in persons may show that their owners are energetic, self-confident and fond of outdoor life. Besides, they may also indicate that they are resourceful, enterprising, active and care little for social conventions. Square finger tips are found in general in persons who are punctual, practical and methodical and who are ruled by reason and custom. Men of smooth fingers and hands are generally impressionable and intuitional. Knotted hands or hands in which joints swell indicate power of analysis, order and reflection in addition to a leaning towards philosophy and scientific speculation.

The forefinger is associated with the planet Jupiter, the middle with that of Saturn, the ring with that of Apollo and the little with that of Mercury. So from the modifications and shapes of the fingers and the temperamental indications of the planets relating to them, we may predict a good deal about the individuals concerned.

The THUMB is the most important and valuable in the science of palmistry. The three phalanges beginning from the top indicate respectively will, reason and love. When the hand is held open *without restraint* and if the forefinger and the middle finger are furthest apart, we may suggest independence of thought in him who owns that hand. If when the hand is held open without restraint, the ring finger and the little finger are widest apart, independence of action may be suggested. In both the above cases, the intervals when they tend to show a wide space, indicate self-reliance and originality. If the thumb inclines inwards towards the other fingers, then the man would be avaricious. If it inclines outwards the quality of generosity may be deduced.

The PALM OF THE HAND has plateaus usually seven in number some more prominent than others. In the hands of some persons these may be clearly represented while in others they may even be entirely absent. Four out of the seven plateaus referred to above lie at the bases of the fingers and are named after the planets applicable to those fingers mentioned already. Of the remaining three, the Mount of Mars comes midway down the palm just beneath the Mount of Mercury. Below that of Mars nearer to the wrist comes the Mount of Luna. The Mount or plateau of Venus lies opposite to that of Luna at the base of the thumb. If the Mount of Jupiter be well developed, we may safely predict in the person the qualities of laudable ambitions and religious connections. If it be poorly developed or absent it would indicate irreligion, idleness and vulgarity. Very excessive development of this mount would moreover indicate love of power, pride and superstitious, or religious fanaticism.

In the science of palmistry the lines of the hand are not at all the most important as many are inclined to think. But lines may give actual indications of actual events to come. Of the many lines of the hand the principal are the lines of life, of head, of heart and of fate. The lines of fortune and fame, of health and of intuition are also valuable. The bracelets of health, wealth and happiness are not to be neglected.

Generally, a 'good' line must be deep, narrow and of good colour. On the other hand, a line broad, shallow, undefined and of indeterminate direction negates the good point that might otherwise be indicated. Breaks, stars and masses of cross lines have special significance.

The old custom of studying only the left hand has been found to be defective and a study of both the hands, first individually, and then in conjunction is at present in favour. The left hand, is said to indicate the inherited and the right hand the modified fortunes of an individual. The contradicting indications of the right hand over the left show the modifications of his fortunes by the change in his character.

Persons with short fingers are usually impulsive and are guided more by instinct rather than by their reason. Persons with short fingers but long nails have a sharp perception and grasp a subject quickly. They are usually averse to wasting time over details. But persons with short fingers and small nails while having an equally sharp perception would allow details though disliking them.

Long fingers indicate a slower judgment after hearing details and after great reasoning. They hear both sides of a question and consequently their conclusions are more unprejudiced and accurate. Small nails indicate critical faculty, methodical work and organizing power especially where the joints are well developed.

Taking the fingers in order, the FIRST OR FOREFINGER is that of Jupiter and a more than normal length of it shows Jupiterian characteristics in the person for that hand. Its three phalanges beginning with the first nail phalange indicate religion, ambition and love of rule.

The SECOND FINGER is that of Saturn, and its three phalanges connote mysticism or melancholy, love of outdoor pursuits and material longings, the last being more emphasised since Saturn is the planet ruling the earth.

The THIRD is the finger of Apollo or Sun and shows a cheerful, bright, optimistic and sunny character. Also the possession of artistic talents is indicated. The first phalange indicates excess in hopefulness, the second if well developed indicates reason or caution and the third ostentation and vulgarity.

The LITTLE FINGER—that of Mercury—is regarded as giving infallible indications of a person's disposition and temper. It signifies remembrance of either a good or bad turn done, for a great length of time. A little finger which is short indicates transitory impulsiveness —quick to take offence and rapid in cooling down. Gratitude for a good turn is equally easily roused and also fades with equal rapidity.

A long first phalange of Mercury indicates flow of language and retentive power for facts. A long second phalange shows perseverance in the face of obstacles and final triumph. A long third phalange indicates contemptible characteristics such as cunning, deceit and dishonesty.

The lines, it has been said, must be deep, clear and even. This indicates continuous and forcible characteristics. Breaks in the lines, and differences in depth of colour indicate lack of purpose and intensity. Lines that branch off in their course show indications of the individual's attempts at a change in his general character. A continuous line but without constant depth of colour would show that the purpose of the individual has varied at different periods. A line dividing and then reuniting shows the resistance of the individual but it is being finally overcome.

There are few cases without the life-line. Such persons may be inferred to have no robust constitution and their life may end at any time. In this case a very strong head line which indicates powerful will, can outweigh the weakness of the life and ensure its continuity. When the life-line mounts high only on the hand from the Mount of Jupiter, it shows a very ambitious life with strong desires, the nature of which is determined by the dominant fingers and mounts. If it runs in, close to the thumb, preventing the Mount of Venus, then the person is cold, unsympathetic and lacking in his desire for relationship with the other sex. When it mounts up in the other direction well into the palm, warmth, passion, generosity and other emotional characteristics may be inferred. A long life-line only denotes the general vigour and natural health of the person and so weakness of the head and heart lines would not ensure long life. A thin, narrow life-line indicates not ill-health or weakness but less capacity for resistance to hardships and exposure. On the other hand, a broad and shallow life-line would signify lack of strength and vigour.

A head-line running up to the Mount of Mercury shows excessive love of money and a stingy nature, while if it runs up to Luna a brilliant imagination may be inferred.

If the heart-line drops very near the head-line, it shows a tendency on the part of the mental faculties to govern the affections. A short heart-line invariably shows a growing selfishness and coldness and may ultimately lead to a failure of affections and even to a deadening of the heart.

An individual who has a strong head-line invariably possesses an equally strong line of fate since the mind is the architect of fortune or fate.

The line of fortune is sometimes called the line of Apollo since it rises up to that mount. One who has this line is marked by some sort of brilliancy such as fame.

The health-line like the life-line shows an individual's constitution and hence is able to throw light on the length of his life.

The four mounts at the bases of the four fingers bear the names of the fingers themselves. That at the base of the thumb is Venus. We have also Mars and the Moon on either side of the palm below Mercury. The last is the Martian Mount and is along that of Venus within the life-line. Those in whom the Mount of Jupiter is prominent have marked Jupiterian qualities, to wit, capacity of being a leader. Saturnine qualities are, as it were, an escapement for the other qualities, being useful in regulating them. It also indicates a sort of cynic sceptic student. Apollo would indicate a warm, healthy, genial, lovable nature with aesthetic tastes. Mercurians have a tireless energy with a keen shrewdness but run the risk of becoming deceptive fraudulent persons. Mars always shows fighting qualities. The Moon indicates weak, nervous, restless persons. When Venus is dominant, it shows a very sympathetic, generous, warm nature capable of loving intensely and causing others to love them.

The hands should first be studied in isolation and then together. To begin with it is best to study the personality of the individual and mark the impression. Such observations as the shapes of the fingers, the nails, the joints, etc., would greatly aid investigations. Then the left hand has to be studied, which, it must be borne in mind, would only indicate the character of the person given him by heredity. Next a study of the right hand must be made which gives his character as modified by his own life and the change in his character. Finally, the two must be studied together which would give a real estimate.

ABHINAYAKKĀḶAI, I.E., 'THE BULL THAT ACTS'

It is a well-known fact that there are more beggars in India than in other parts of the world and the reason for this is, that the Indians generally pay more attention to the development of finer instincts than the people of other countries. Fellow feeling and the feeling of humanity are the characteristics that deserve cultivation in every human being was the motive that prompted the origin of various charitable institutions in India. Fellow beings are helped not so much because they are in difficulties and wants, but because it helps the donor to bestow on charity more and more freely and heartily each time than before. Only from this standpoint certain people object to the proposal of putting a sort of check over the community of beggars and thus free the people from their molestations. Deprive a land of its beggars and you deprive its people of one of their opportunities of drawing out their innate feeling of humanity and pity.

To draw the attention and enlist the sympathy of the people the beggars devised various methods. Some assumed the guises of sufferers from loathsome diseases, to wit, leprosy and so forth. Some contrived to appear lame or blind or deformed, to move the people to pity. Some had trained animals like monkeys, bears and dogs whose antics and trained actions procured them their daily livelihood. Serpents with their fangs drawn out and giant scorpions with their stings rendered harmless by being dipped into acids, etc., are common sights one can see in the land in the possession of certain beggars going around the cities and villages in their daily avocations. Similarly there arose a class of beggars, and they went by the name of 'Beggars in possession of *Abhinayakkāḷai*'. They belonged to a nomadic set of people and wandered from place to place. They earned their living by begging and one or more trained bulls were their companions in begging. Just as a trained monkey is made to exhibit before the people its performances, like jumping over a bar of wood or passing through an iron ring by its master, these trained bulls are made to show by their actions at the command of their masters that they understand what is required of them. In fact the present day display in a circus may be said to be an improvement on the above practice on a very large scale. There instead of one trained animal helping a poor beggar to get a few pence, a number of trained animals help the rich proprietor of a menagerie to make huge profits. Further, instead of the performer going from house to house, the people go to the place where the performance takes place. The animals, instead of being put on their routine a number of times, exhibit their skill only once before a large audience.

The owner of the *Abhinayakkāḷai*, having decked it in embroidered cloths, tinsels and glass beads, takes it to different houses and he generally has a crowd of urchins belonging to the village at his heels. He puts several questions to it and it nods its head once, twice and so on to indicate that its answer is in the affirmative or the negative. At times a cow is also taken along with it and the two are made to play the part of lovers. By clever management a series of incidents in lovers' quarrels are enacted before the delighted audience, the two animals playing the part of lovers at quarrel. The *coup de grace* to the performance is the way in which the lovers make up their differences and caress each other to show that they are sweet lovers once more ! !

In certain organized villages itinerant beggars, who frequent them only periodically and at long intervals, go at first to the village headman. He fixes the quantity of grain to be paid to him from each house. Generally a chalk mark is made inside the small measure the beggar has and people fill it with grain up to the mark made. In this way the work, both of the villagers and the beggar is made easy. The beggar will not be able to trouble the innocent villagers and squeeze as much grain as he possibly could, which, the beggars bringing wild animals like bears with them often did. They in fact used in former days not to quit the front of a particular house unless and until a certain quantity of rice demanded by them was paid to them.

It is a noteworthy fact that in interior villages, where the children are denied the sight of even very ordinary wild animals like bears, the visit of beggars with them is hailed with delight ; and they generally reaped a fine reward especially in those days of peace and plenty. Further, it is a well-known fact that bears break up anthills and suck in swarms of ants, especially white ants, and the villagers, whose houses were made the residences and play-houses of these tiny pests, eagerly watched for the arrival of beggars with bears to be rid of the white ants and the harm done to them and to their furniture, etc.

Thus it will be seen that barring the beggars, who are veritable parasites living upon the labours of others, there are others who do at least something to deserve the alms bestowed on them either by their songs, toys like rattles made of palm leaves which, they give in exchange for handfuls of rice or by showing different kinds of snakes and wild animals to the rustic boys and girls. The last ones, perhaps, do what the menageries in big cities are intended to do, though on a very poor scale.

GIPSIES

Gipsies belong to a wandering race supposed to be of Hindu origin with dark skin and hair, living by basket-making, horse-dealing, fortune-telling and other allied methods. They speak a very corrupt form of Hindi in the northern parts of India. This race, when it first appeared in England in the early sixteenth century, they were supposed to have come from Egypt and even now this race of people goes by the name of 'Egyptian Gipsy race', perhaps from the name of the country they originally came from. The language spoken by the European Gypsies is called Romany. In general terms this Gipsy race is described as a vagabond race whose tribes coming originally from India entered Europe in the fourteenth or fifteenth century and are now scattered over Turkey, Russia, Hungary, Spain, England, etc., living by theft, fortune-telling, horse-jockeying, tinkering and so on. Further reference reveals to us the fact that this race of vagabond tribes are scattered over North America and even along the northern coast of Africa in addition to the countries in Europe and the greater part of Asia.

The language of Gipsies being called Romany from the word *Rom* which means a man or husband. There are some who connect this word *Rom* with the name of the Indian God Rāma. But the explanation identifying the name with *Doma* or *Domba* the Sanskrit expression for a low-caste musician appears to be more reasonable. Though innumerable tribes of Gipsies have been described, the Indian tribes of Gipsies alone may be considered. The thieves of different countries, are supposed to have a jargon of their own and as Gipsy tribes had some such dialects among them, they may be catalogued under thieves which they were and are—at least most of them—even at the present day.

It is a fact acknowledged on all hands that Gipsies wandered forth from India, but the question of 'when' and 'from what part or parts' has not been satisfactorily answered. But the fact remains that some connect the word *Rom* referred to above with the Indian dialects and go to the extent of deriving it from languages such as Hindi, Marathi, and so on.

Whatever may be the character of these tribes of itinerant beggars, the fact remains that they professed to possess certain miraculous powers, and people—and at times very rich and influential people too—have gone to the extent of consulting them not only in times of difficulties but also on ordinary occasions to obtain information as to the possible success or failure of certain undertakings they were engaged in. There have also been instances recorded in which bachelors and maids have consulted them as to their future wives and husbands, to wit, their social status, temperament and so on.

Wanderers from place to place without any fixed place of residence, they stole away not only cattle but also children with impunity in bygone unsettled days. In spite of their evil reputation, it may be said, that these people, or at least many of them, did possess certain mysterious powers and people believed in them.

It is a fact that the Tōḍas living on the Nilgiris do possess even certain miraculous powers. Even to-day lads in their teens have, it seems, the peculiar power to hypnotize birds by gazing at them and to catch them without the use of snares or bird-lime. They say that any one who cares to approach them might, by tactful management, verify at least the above statement.

People belonging to certain hill tribes are believed to possess certain roots and the possession of which is considered to secure for those possessing them immunity from the dangers of lightning. Certain roots are said to have the power of fascinating cat-family to wit tigers, leopards and so on. The root of a plant called *Poonai Vanaṅgi* when placed in the room of a house, would make the cats stick to that room for hours together !! An old woman gathering twigs in a forest is said to have been given by a mountaineer a small quantity of a root to eat, which secured for her immunity from the pangs of hunger and thirst for many days ! Having so many recorded evidences of miraculous powers possessed by certain sects of people, we may even go to the extent of believing in the powers which at least certain Gipsies in certain places did possess and won the confidence of the people they came in contact with. It is but true that the majority of Gipsies found nowadays scattered over the countries do not possess any such powers and that they are thieves and rogues in the guise of beggars. But many of them in bygone days appear to have won the esteem and confidence of the people by the exhibition of certain wonderful powers they possessed by way of fortune-telling and so on. As people who possess mysterious powers are generally reticent to exhibit the same to others, people interested in such things may do well to satisfy themselves.

It is a noteworthy fact that Gipsies, exercising influence over the other people, are invariably dressed in piebald robes. It may be for the purpose of attracting attention or inspiring the credulous with awe or it may have something to do with hypnotism itself. People are considered to be under the influence of different planets and each planet is supposed to have its own colour. In hypnotizing men and animals, men in the know make use of different colours to influence different people according to their temperament. The precious stones are considered to possess extraordinary power in this direction and hence ancient magicians are said to have used emeralds, rubies, corals, pearls, diamonds, saphires, etc., to influence people. Such being the case, these people in the absence of costly gems might have found cloths of different colours tolerably helpful for the purpose of influencing men and animals. Instead of wearing a ring set with different kinds of precious stones, they might be wearing a piebald dress or dress formed of patches of cloths of diverse hues.

Another noteworthy point in dealing with the subject of Gipsies is the fact that many of them carry a taboret called in Tamil *Uḍukku* and use it when invoking the aid of invisible beings or elementals. As the Hindus believe in the potency of harmonious sounds and music in invoking the presence of good elementals and employ musicians on all auspicious occasions, and, as they make use of certain strains of music on funeral occasions when one is dead, it may be safely concluded that the sounding of the taboret by Gipsies may be either for the purpose of imposing upon the audience or for genuine hypnotic purposes. We all know that sound sooths as in the illustrations of snakes and children charmed by the music and lulled to sleep by lullabies respectively. It also rouses the passions and emotions of men as is evinced by the play of martial strains of music in battle fields. Hence the taborets used by Gipsies may be for the purpose of effecting certain results.

COSTUME WEARING

It is a well-known fact that people in different countries wear different costumes. By a mere glance at the costume worn by a lady in Europe one can say the nationality to which she belongs. In the same way the ladies in Southern India dress in different ways in different communities. The *Smārta* ladies, the *Vaishnava* ladies and the ladies of the *Telugu*-speaking community have each a distinguishing mode of wearing their costumes, and by looking at them even from a distance we can say the community to which she belongs. The *Āndhras* from the Telugu districts have their own peculiar mode of dressing, and the other settlers in Southern India from Guzarat, Bombay and other places have their own special distinguishing mode of dressing to distinguish them from the people of the other communities.

It is, no doubt, true that climatic conditions of countries have contributed very largely to the varying modes of dressing by men and women there. But let us see whether any other reason or reasons can be assigned for the different modes of dressing in different countries and in different communities.

It is probable that when different organizers of communities and sects desired to hit upon a plan by which any one belonging to his community or sect could be singled out from among the rest, it struck him that a change in the mode of the dress might effectively serve his purpose. So he invented perhaps certain innovations, simple in the beginning, differing but little from the mode of dress adopted by them till then, which in course of time grew into distinct communal or sectional costumes.

The orthodox Hindus and especially the Brāhmins of Southern India attach a sort of religious importance to the mode of dress and this importance is emphasized during the observance of religious and other ceremonies. A bridegroom should at the time of performing the marriage ceremony and ever afterwards subsequently wear his costumes in *Pañchakachcham* meaning five folds of the lower garment tucked into the waist band or *Kachchai*. The number five is considered to be a very sacred number as evinced from the study of the derivation of the expressions *Pañcha-Gavyam*, *Pañcha-Bhūtam*, *Pañchāngam*, *Pañcha-Agni* and so on. In this connection the word *Pañcha-Kōsa* appears to be worthy of notice. The human soul is said to be wearing five '*Kōsas*' or garments (bodies) one over and above the other and the magnetic force radiating from it has to pass through from the higher of these bodies to the lower through certain portions of the bodies or garments. This is always taking place in the higher bodies and when the force or magnetism comes to the coarsest of these bodies—the physical body—it is highly desirable that it is not frittered away into the surrounding air but is kept circulating in the body itself.

Every tyro in science knows about the action of points. The Hindu sages of old were thoroughly conversant with the play of forces like electricity and magnetism and in order to make the people of those days (especially the orthodox Brāhmins, who were every moment accumulating in their bodies animal magnetism) not to lose much of it or in other words to minimise its loss. Hence they had laid it down as a religious obligation to wear the costume in a particular manner so that the points or folds tucked in, may, by the action of points, discharge the magnetic and other forces in a manner highly advantageous for the individual concerned. This very same argument applies equally to the garments worn by the orthodox Indian ladies. At any rate, edges or corners of garments hanging out exposed to air and thus becoming capable of discharging out uselessly by the action of points the accumulated force is condemned by the Indian saints and sages. In fact, the sages and *Yōgis* of old had held that there was a greater loss of human magnetic force when wearing garments than when not wearing them. They hold that through the tips of fingers and toes enough force is wasted to benefit the unseen matter as intended by nature and those that care to minimize the loss to their high advantage may dress themselves as laid down in the *Dharma Sāstras.*

An orthodox Hindu would not send the cloth he has once worn for a time to the laundry and in fact he holds that he should himself wash his clothes daily and wear them. It is also said to be laid down in the *Sāstras* that the clothes worn by an individual should not be worn by others and the beds and vessels like drinking cups, etc., of one should not be made use of by others. The ostensible reason for this injunction may be to avoid the possibility of communication of infectious diseases. The man wearing a garment may be suffering from an infectious disease, say, like syphilis and if others use it they may catch the loathsome disease. Similarly a bed or a drinking cup may transmit to others the microbes carrying infection with them. But religion goes further and says that the garments, beds and drinking cups used by one if used by others are productive of other kinds of harm in addition to those noticed above. Germs affecting the morals of individuals are likely to be inoculated in the system by wearing the garments, etc., of others. A man strengthening his magnetism by religious observances need not necessarily be pure morally and hence his clothes, etc., saturated with his magnetism may also be steeped in his germs of moral vices and thus capable of affecting the others wearing them most injuriously.

At any rate, the Hindu sages had held that the use of clothes was not only to serve the purpose of hiding the nakedness of mankind, but also to serve other religious and scientific purposes also. Instead of brushing aside as superstitious belief this opinion of the ancient sages, one would do well to make experiments that might suggest themselves to him and satisfy himself as to the truth contained in the statements.

KARAKAM (WATER POT) CARRYING

EVERY village in India is considered to be under the protection and patronage of a deity named *Sāstha* or *Ayyanār*. This deity has a temple and is often propitiated by the villagers by the offerings of worship, sacrifices and so on. Any villager could take a vow to take the village guardian deity in procession through the streets of the village if the particular business he is engaged in ends in success, or he may do the same to propitiate the deity to do him and his good generally. The deity is carried through the streets of the village only during nights and all the other minor deities are considered to be afraid of him. In fact he is the suzerain lord of the super-physical entities just as the village headman is of its people.

Some of the minor deities by some cause or other get displeased with the whole village or particular people in the village. Then they vent their wrath by causing epidemics among the villagers, their cattle or their produce. To avert the evil the villagers carry the *Ayyanār* through the streets in procession at nights with burning torches and the beating of tom-toms and trumpets. The deity stops in front of each of the houses and the inmates offer him incense, fruits, halves of just then broken cocoanuts and burning camphor. The deity is taken back to the temple generally at a very late hour.

This peculiar custom appears to be special for India; since so far as ascertained no other country appears to be following or to have followed this custom.

In villages composed of flesh eaters, if the ravages of the epidemics appear to be rather heavy and the tolls taken alarming, sheep and even buffaloes are slaughtered at the corners of the streets and boiled rice mixed with the blood of the slaughtered animals is made into balls and thrown in all directions high up in the sky and the people believe that in former days those balls of rice never fell to the ground as they were caught and devoured by the minor entities or spirits! Some think that even now in some villages the balls of rice soaked in the blood of the slaughtered victims and thrown into the sky at dead of night would never reach the earth!! When the practice referred to above is to be followed in any particular village, the *Poosāri* or the man usually worshipping the deity every day gives timely previous notice to the villagers of the same, warning them not to come outside but to remain indoors after 12 o'clock at night till the procession has passed their streets, lest they should come to grief since people who witness the process, generally get frightened which in many cases might result in death.

Akin to the practices referred to above, there is the custom of carrying *Karakam* or pot containing water and decorated with margosa leaves, flowers, sandal paste, lime fruit, etc. When any epidemic is virulent in any village, one or more *Karakams* are carried through the streets of the village on the heads of people, specially chosen for the purpose, who must bathe and keep clean and pure for the nonce. The popular belief is that this carrying in procession of the *Karakam* or *Karakams* checks the virulence of the epidemic, though it may not avert calamity forthwith.

In auspicious religious ceremonies, the Hindus place a pot of water over paddy spread on the ground, swept and washed clean and decorated. A cluster of mango leaves is placed over the pot and on it a cocoanut is placed. After the chant of certain *mantras* or incantations the water is said to become possessed of special properties, being magnetized perhaps by the above processes. It is then distributed in small quantities to be taken in and it is also sprinkled over the persons or things to purify them.

In auspicious religious ceremonies malevolent and evil spirits would not be invoked by the people. Hence it stands to reason that the pot of water is intended to invoke the presence of benevolent and good spirits only. Hence the *Karakam* should have hovering over it only good spirits. Then how is it that the evil spirits the promoters of epidemics generally, are exorcised and driven from the various points of the villages when *Karakams* are carried through them? It must be due to the presence of these good spirits whose influence radiating from them is perhaps uncongenial to the evil spirits to remain in their positions of vantage any longer. They are scared away even as a bear is scared away by a lighted match. Evening twilight is the time most favourable for carrying the *Karakam* in procession, since only then the spirits are considered to have special power.

When houses are being built, a kind of melon called *Sāmbal Poosunikāi* (white pumpkin) is kept suspended in front of the house to scare away undesirable spirits who might otherwise enter the premises and cause harm to the owners of the buildings and at times to the builders themselves. It might be asked as to why these evil spirits did not enter there before. The reason perhaps is that they do not like orderly and inhabited places and prefer only ruined or uninhabited places. When a house is being demolished the evil spirits hasten thither. But the melon resembling a big egg full of water or juice has the power to frighten them away. Perhaps this vegetable has the same power which the *Karakams* have with this difference that in the former case evil spirits are prevented from entering the house under construction while in the latter case the streets are rid of their presence.

KĀVAḌI-BEARING

Of the many singular Indian customs the one going by the name *Kāvaḍi*-bearing, deserves notice. The word itself appears to be the combination of two words *Kāvu* and *aḍi* intended to mean the vow made to walk the distance to the place of pilgrimage on foot. There are different kinds of this *Kāvaḍi* and of which three are worth mentioning.

There is one going by the name of *Annakāvaḍi*. It consists in the devotee going from house to house begging for cooked rice not with the idea of satisfying his own hunger, but to offer the gathering to God. An offering to God generally means an offering to humanity. Hence the vow of taking *Annakāvaḍi* is really a vow to beg food from others, going from door to door and place to place, and to offer the same to the hungry and needy in God's name. Nowadays this principle is lost sight of and we have in the place of this beautiful and fine custom a degenerated one of selfishness. People have begun to entertain the belief that living a life of laziness after satisfying the hunger with the food obtained by begging would bring them nearer to God. The second kind of *Kāvaḍi* is called the *Pāl-Kāvaḍi* or the vow of begging for milk from house to house to be utilized in the service of God. Usually the milk collected is poured upon the image of the deity, collected again in a vessel and disposed of either by distributing it among the children or by utilizing the same for satisfying personal hunger and demand.

The third variety of *Kāvaḍi* is perhaps the one observed by people without the possibility of its degenerating into selfish use in the end. It consists in making a vow that he or she would make a pilgrimage to the one or the other of the temples to worship the deity there. It is nothing but the offering of the devotee's energy to the deity. In the elementary stage it consists in walking to the temple of the deity ; but in advanced stages it was intended to mean the use of the individual's energy in the service of God which means the service of humanity as evinced from the fact that a *Samārādhana* or feeding of the people is performed after all such observance of vows, though in some cases people may not find it convenient to perform it.

There is a philosophical and spiritual side to all observances of Hindu religious rites, ceremonies and customs. Here also we have an interesting philosophical and spiritual principle involved in the custom and the *Kāvaḍi* carried to the temple gives us an idea of it.

The wise sages who originated the custom wanted to make the observance of it interesting. A man in a village might have taken this vow of *Kāvaḍi* which strictly means the sacrifice of a walk to the temple. He might have walked to the temple several times after the taking of the vow and may wish to set off one such walk against the promised one to the deity, and thus the spirit needed may be lost sight of. So an object called *Kāvaḍi* in the form of a segment of a circle was made, decorated and carried to the temple with great veneration to instil in the mind of the observer the right spirit needed.

As all religious rites appeal to invisible worlds, the *Kāvaḍi* is the fittest form to represent the blessings in the invisible world through the mercy of the invisible deity who for ever eludes our grasp.

The origin of *Kāvaḍi*-bearing is said to be that God Siva at one time gave in Mount Kāilas to sage Agastya, the dwarfish sage, two hillocks for being taken to his abode in the south of India for worship in his place and that of His consort. But the sage left them there in a forest and returned to the south. When at another time he was about to start to the north with the set object of bringing these two divine hillocks, his disciple Iḍumban, offered to carry them himself. Accordingly, Iḍumban proceeded to the forest following the directions given by his master. When he was at a loss to know how to lift them, the *Daṇḍa* or stick of Brahma stood over the hillocks while the snakes of the earth served in place of ropes to enable him to carry them, duly fastened to the rod. He thereupon lifted them, bore them on his shoulders and brought them to the south. While nearing the forest near Paḷni in Diṇḍigal Taluk, he kept them on the ground to rest a while. On attempting to lift them again, he found them to his surprise permanently fixed to the ground at that spot !

To know the reason thereof, he got over them and there he noticed a youth with a stick in one hand and wearing only underwear. On being questioned as to why the hillocks would not move, he claimed them as his own ; then an altercation ensued with the result that Iḍumban fell senseless in the scuffle. Recovering from the swoon and recognizing in the boy the divine Subrahmanya, Iḍumban prayed to him that those offering vows bearing *Kāvaḍi* similar to the one adopted by him in bringing these sacred hillocks, should be blessed fully and relieved from all difficulties. This was granted which accounts for the bearing of *Kāvaḍi* by Hindus on all important festive occasions. The subject is fully dealt with in the *South Indian Festivities* under the head ' SKANDA SASHTI ' and in the *South Indian Shrines* in the chapter on ' PALNI '.

YELLOW ROBES

MOST of the Hindu customs have behind them rational bases and consequently do not deserve to be brushed aside as useless, and born of ignorance and superstition. From the simplest to the most complicated customs of the Hindus, to wit, from their mode of dress to the performance of elaborate sacrifices, festivals, rites and ceremonies, there is not one but admits of explanation, both rational and acceptable.

Though the mode of dressing of the majority of the present day heterodox Hindus has completely changed, yet there are a few orthodox Hindu men and women in remote corners of obscure villages far away from the din and bustle of modern civilization who still adhere to the old habits of their forefathers, among many other things, even in the mode of their dress. The ladies, though poor, would not wear a cloth unless it contains at least a small percentage of silk thread in it. The men struggling hard to make both ends meet, would not wear a cloth devoid of borders of silk thread. Why do they cling to this custom with a tenacity worthy of better causes one may be tempted to ask. The answer from the simple-minded wearer, if at all given, would fill the mind of the questioner with wonder at the profound wisdom of the ancients and serve the purpose of an eye-opener if it is not thoroughly prejudiced, beyond the possibility of easy openness and flexibility.

The explanation for the custom may, perhaps, be highly scientific verging on the question of the preservation of human magnetism and so on. As these forces are invisible and not tangible, ordinary people could not understand the invaluable benefit which a few threads at least of silk in a piece of woven cloth would confer on its wearer.

The use of the BIRKENHEAD FILTER could not be understood by the laymen, nay, even by many of the educated, unless until the sediment left after the process of filtration, opens their eyes to the quantity of dirt swallowed and taken into the system, by men using water considered satisfactorily pure. A doctor would never use the ordinary water from the tap to prepare his mixture for his patient, since he knows how impure it is. Similarly the sages of old knew the nature of the invisible forces of nature and their effect on men, animals and plants. They designed the various customs to serve the purpose of utilizing these forces as best as they could for human advantage. So we may proceed on the assumption that the yellow coloured robes worn by *Brahmachāris* (lads for whom the thread-wearing ceremony has been duly performed) and newly married couples of the Hindus can disclose certain set purpose. Why the dye yellow of all the dyes, is selected to colour the robes in? It is because yellow colour symbolizes intellect and a *Brahmachāri* and a *Grihasta* begin to develop it after *Upadēsam* or initiation in the way of doing it.

A man is a centre having within it several centres in communication with the cosmic centres. Each of these cosmic centres is responsible for the flash of a certain colour in the solar light or human bodies, both visible and invisible. Human will is the switch-board to connect or disconnect the circuit of micro-cosmic centres or the centres in man with the micro-cosmic ones. One switch colours the human body formed of finer invisible stuff yellow, another rosy-red, and so on. This is mentioned in the *Upanishads* of the Hindus. So the yellow robe worn symbolizes the fact that the individual has just been instructed in the use of a particular switch in the switch-board, if he is a *Brahmachāri*. The yellow robes worn by married couples symbolize the fact that they together are beginning to tread the pathway of wisdom or knowledge of the Supreme.

Further, colours in flowers serve the purpose of attracting insects to facilitate the process of seed formation, bringing about the union of the 'pistil' and the 'pollen.' Similarly, colours serve the purpose of attracting desirable or undesirable beings of the super-physical worlds. The yellow robes attract denizens of the finer worlds to those wearing them. Their presence and the vibrations radiating from them, help such in the attempts they make at the progress towards the goal of attaining supreme knowledge. What is now considered beyond human ken, was within the experience of lads of six and seven in bygone spiritual age! The ebb of the materialistic wave is sure to bring in its wake the old order of things when every Hindu custom will be revived and welcomed as a boon conferred on humanity by the wise sages of old.

MUDIVĀṄGAL, I.E., REMOVING HAIR

In many of the families of Southern India a peculiar custom is being observed. As soon as a child is born, its hair is offered or rather promised to the deity in one or other of the temples where such offerings are commonly given. Even grown-up men and women among the Hindus, excepting those in the Brāhmin community, have their heads close shaven if at all they happen to pay a visit to one or other of such places. Thousands and thousands of children and grown-up men and women visit places like Vaithīsvarankōil in the district of Tanjore, Paḷni near Madura, Tiruvallūr near Madras, the famous Tirupati and so on, and offer their hair as a sacrifice to the deity.

This time-worn custom has intense merit not because of the object sacrificed, but because of the spirit and religious fervour with which the offering is made. After all God, who is all-powerful and who has created the whole universe, and everything contained in it, does not care so much for the objects offered; but the spirit with which the sacrifice is made makes all the difference. At first sight it might appear to a critic that an offering to the deity of such a worthless overgrowth, perhaps of hair, is an insult and not an object of merit; but mature consideration would surely change his angle of vision.

A maiden, whose beauty perhaps, lies in her wealth of hair cheerfully and gladly lays it at the altar of the Almighty and this spirit has in it the germ of a mightier sacrifice she will be ready and willing to make at a future time, when called upon to do so. She puts up with the feeling of shame she naturally feels in appearing before other people, ugly with a close-shaven head, in the belief that she has done the act to please God. Who could say that this feeling of divine service is not a noble feeling? Moreover the standard of offering to the God should be the same for the rich and the poor. Other kinds of offerings can be made only by the fortunate few, but this offering of the hair might be made by one and all, both high and low, rich and poor, male and female. If the offering comes from the depths of the heart, no other offering, however costly it might be, would be considered equal to this by the deity.

This custom has, perhaps, been originated by the wise men of bygone days and so it deserves examination. By selecting such an offering to the God, they, perhaps, intended to teach the people the lesson that the nature of the offering to the God does not count, but the spirit with which the offering was made, certainly made it noble or ignoble.

It is an acknowledged fact in the tenets of Hindu religion that the service of humanity is the service of God. This simple offering has in it the deepest meaning and possibility, namely, 'LOVE OF HUMANITY AND SERVICE TO IT,' if one but rightly understands it and follows it in the right spirit.

In this connection it may be mentioned that a large number of people are usually fed after the performance of any *Prārthana* (vow of religious offering) which clearly supports the statement made, namely, 'SERVICE OF HUMANITY IS SERVICE OF GOD.'

SACRED ANIMALS AND PLANTS

Of the many queer customs and beliefs prevalent among the Hindus this may be found interesting and worthy of deep consideration. A really good and pious Hindu would not dare to do certain actions forbidden by the sacred laws going by the name *Dharma Sāstras* of Manu whose duty it was to lay down rules for the different Hindu communities to follow and which no Hindu should transgress. It has been laid down by this law-giver to people that certain pests, like parrots, rabbits and so forth that cause a good deal of loss to the ryots, may be destroyed. Certain animals and plants, though causing trouble to people, are considered sacred and hence should not be destroyed. Among animals, the cow, the cat, the squirrel, the monkey, the brāhmani-kite, etc., are considered sacred; and from among the vegetable kingdom, the *Asvatta* tree (*Ficus religiosa*), the cocoanut tree, the bael tree, the *Tuḷasi* plant (*Ocymum sanctum*), etc. are considered holy and hence should not be destroyed. A pious Hindu would rather let an *Asvatta* tree continue to grow on the wall of his house or in a crevice of the rampart round the well in his garden than destroy it. He would not dare to cut down cocoa-nut trees to clear a place for house-building.

The principle or sentiment underlying the custom is based on certain reasons that do not deserve to be brushed aside as superstitious. Accumulated experiences of years of ages have taught the people this principle or sentiment, by whatever name one may choose to call it, and hence we may with advantage try to understand its rationale.

It has been an acknowledged fact everywhere in the world that the lives of men are of graded importance. A king should be protected even at the sacrifice of innumerable men. The life of a General in the army is more precious than the lives of many other inferior officers in the regiment. There is a quotation in the *Nīti Sāstras* (ethical codes) of the Hindus, the general import of which is that even in a family, the lives of its members are considered to be of graded importance. When once this is grasped and the principle conceded, then the rationale under reference will become intelligible. The Hindu law-giver, Manu, has laid down that the life of a Brāhmin is many times more precious than the life of a Kshatriya, a Vaisya or a Sūdra and the reason for the same is, that a really true Brāhmin has really nothing personal and everything he has and every action he does are for the benefit of humanity at large. So it goes without saying that he should be preserved even at the sacrifice of many a selfish people, self-centred and living on the labours of others like so many parasites on other trees and plants. The same is the case in the animal and in the vegetable kingdoms also. There are plants that are veritable benefactors of men and animals. By their very existence, they purify the atmosphere and create healthy surroundings for the animals to live in good health. The destruction of one of such trees or plants would mean the deprival of a portion of the benefit which the animals were enjoying. It has been said that a man exhausted by mental strain would recuperate his vitality and strength, if he would but go to a cocoanut tope and remain there seated for a time, leaning against one of the trees. The same or different advantageous properties may be found in other trees and plants held sacred by the Hindu sages of old. The ban put on certain vegetables such as onions, etc., may be due to hygienic and various other reasons. Only with this object in view, the destruction of certain animals and plants is considered sinful by the pious orthodox Hindus and this in consequence accounts for the Indians considering certain animals and plants sacred.

SLEEPING POSTURES

HINDUS always go to sleep with their heads turned towards the south or towards east, and this immemorial practice finds support in the *Purānas—Mārkandēya* and *Vishnu* as well as in the *Āhnēga Tattwa*. When the basic principle underlying the custom is properly understood, we find that the profound knowledge of the sages, who insisted on the principle being followed, stands revealed. The majority of the Hindus *believed* and still continue to believe that a violation of this principle may result in ill-health. The *Purānas* and other works, though they hint at such a thing, do not explain the '*why*' of the principle, fearing, perhaps, that doing which will be tantamount to instructing the people in the last words of magic or superscience—very dangerous in the hands of the wicked and the unscrupulous.

Everyone knows that the earth is a huge body magnetized by the force generated by the sun's intense heat. It is also known to all, that the earth is almost round and only one-half of it is exposed to the sun's heat at a time. Thus one portion or other of the earth's surface must always remain hot and hence the earth is always being surcharged with the thermal magnetism. The portion not so exposed must, of course, remain lower in temperature than the part so exposed. Perhaps, this combined with diverse other reasons has made the earth retain different kinds of magnetic force at the different poles. The persistence of a magnetic needle in a compass in assuming a position pointing always the northern direction, however much its equilibrium may be disturbed, fully bears out this truth.

The human body is a magnet, the aggregate red corpuscles which contain a large percentage of iron contributing to it in no small measure. This body has a sphere of influence surrounding and interpenetrating it, just as the earth has of the substance called ether, the medium for such play of forces. It has also the two poles, the positive and the negative, just as the earth has, in the sphere of ether, otherwise called the sphere of electrons. It is said that objects remain on the surface of the earth because of gravity ; but Hindu *yōgis* (sages), who are superscientists, remain suspended in the air against gravity and have given as explanation that the change of polar magnetism in the body by their will-power makes the earth repel them from its surface and hence they easily float in the space.

Normally, the physical body, the child of the earth, maintains the magnetism unlike that of the earth and hence by the scientific dictum, 'LIKE POLES REPEL AND UNLIKE POLES ATTRACT', remains on earth being attracted towards it.

The sun magnetizes the human sphere of ether as well as the earthly sphere of ether. The earth being a huge sphere and the human sphere being a tiny one, the former is influencing the latter every second and the influence is greatest when man lies over the earth, his whole body remaining in contact with it. If the influence is to be beneficial, then a man must lie down and sleep with his head turned towards the south or towards the east. When a man lies down and sleeps, the mighty magnet, the earth, at that time of night when man's vitality is at the lowest level, being deprived of the sun's help, pours into or takes away from man his vitality according to the posture he lies in placing his sphere of ether in a position favourable to receive or to give up vitality.

If we suppose that man's head represents the north

pole and the feet the south pole, and the magnetic and other forces pour from the north pole and flow towards the south, then it stands to reason that the magnetic force flowing over the earth from the north pole, will act in unison with that force flowing from the north pole to the south pole of the sphere in man.

It is an accepted truth that all forces travel in circles and return eventually to the place they started from. The heart sends out good blood and receives back blood saturated with all sorts of impurities. Similarly the forces flowing from the north pole is very pure at first and hence when a portion of it pours into the human sphere by the position it occupies, it results in the man's good health. The forces returning from the south pole is perhaps saturated with all kinds of impure magnetism. A man by lying down with his head turned towards the south, places himself in a position favourable for the flow of impure magnetism into his body. If a man is naturally strong, the flow of force emanating from his body may counteract this flow of impure magnetism and reduce the evil to a minimum. Else ill-health may be the result.

It is also the belief of many that by sleeping with the head placed towards the east, one may be enabled to acquire knowledge by the magnetic and other forces passing over the surface of the earth from east to west tending to stimulate the brain activity in a gentle and healthy way.

The custom of placing a corpse with the head pointed to the south before its cremation takes place tends to show that the vital magnetism in the body is completely extinct and hence it is only fit to be burnt.

It is also allegorically represented in the story of the elephant-headed God, Vināyakar, that one may be deprived of both life and wisdom by sleeping with the head pointing to the north. The story in brief is that

Vināyakar had originally a human head. One day he provoked his father Siva to anger and consequently had his head severed from the trunk under His orders. Pārvati, Siva's consort, begged Siva to restore her her Vināyakar. Siva thereupon directed one of his attendants to go into the forest and bring to him the head of an animal that may happen to be sleeping with the head directed towards the north, meaning thereby that its life is forfeited to Yama. An elephant was found to be sleeping with its head turned towards the north. So its head was severed from its trunk and brought to Siva who placed it with the trunk on Vināyakar and restored him to life! The elephant represents strength and wisdom and it lost both by sleeping with its head to the north. So by sleeping with the head directed towards the north one may lose both life and wisdom, is taught to the people by this story.

DĀNAM, I.E., GIFTS

Of all the nations in the world, it is the Hindus, perhaps, who attach very great importance to gifts. The life of a true Hindu should be one of continuous giving and not grasping. It is ordained in the *Dharma Sāstras* of the Hindus that a portion of the earnings of every man should be set apart and devoted to charity. Looking into the past, we find the ancient Hindu Rājas devoting a large portion of the public money as well as a high percentage of their private money also in charity. Apart from the actions of the Government and the community in this direction during the early ages, the action of individuals and individual families bestowing gifts on important occasions deserves special notice. Instances of these by thousands may be met with in the inscriptions recorded on the stone walls of temples.

In every family, when an *Upanayanam* or thread-wearing ceremony, marriage, *Seemantam* or any other joyous occasion is celebrated, *Bhoori*, *Dhakshana* or whatever name you may give to the gifts bestowed on people on the occasion, plays a very prominent part. In fact, an *Upanayanam* or marriage performed without gifts of money and other things would be an unheard of event in the annals of the Hindus. Free feeding on all festive occasions is a well-known thing and hence needs no comment on it here. But special gifts deserve notice.

Animals such as elephants, horses, cows and even rams are considered suitable objects of gift on all occasions. *Tulābhāra* or the gift of gold and other precious metals or coins equal in weight to the individual is another recognized form of gift. These are not within the reach of ordinary men. Only very rich people can afford to give valuable gifts, like those mentioned above. But there are gifts within reach of even very poor people.

The gift of a cocoanut is considered to be equal in efficacy to the gift of a cow, only in cases where people are too poor to bestow a cow in gift. The gift of sandals, fans, beds, cots, new cloths, ghee, oil, etc., are also considered meritorious. The belief is that the soul after parting from the body at death has to pass through several regions before reaching its destination. The several gifts made while alive made it easy for the soul to cross the several regions on the homeward journey. When an individual is about to die, several gifts are given. Even during the ten days of funeral ceremony, gifts of different kinds are made especially on the tenth day.

A cow given as a gift at the time of an individual's death is said to help that individual's soul in crossing a river called *Vaitharani.* Similarly oil, mirror, etc., are considered to be favourable for the easy passage of the soul over barren deserts and difficulties due to illusions. Fans, cloths, beds, sandals, etc., given as gifts at the time of the death of an individual or shortly after are considered capable of producing on departing souls, comforts akin to those derived while using them when alive. In all cases of gift, the spirit with which it is made is the only thing that counts and not the objects given, is the belief of the learned in bygone days.

PAVITHRAM, I.E., PURIFICATION RING

OF the many unique customs prevalent among the Hindus, the wearing of a *Pavithram*, a kind of ring, made of *kusa* grass on the ring finger of the right hand while performing religious rites and ceremonies deserves notice. The word *Pavithram* means purity. Hence this ring-substitute of *kusa* grass bearing that name implies that the man performing the rites and ceremonies becomes purified for the nonce by wearing it. In fact physical purity, as well as emotional and mental, are considered highly essential for the success in the performances of such rites and ceremonies. Hence previous to the commencement of all such religious ceremonies, people observing them, bathe in rivers, tanks or any reservoir of water to obtain physical purity. As an apology for emotional purity they either fast or live on lighter diet at least for a day or a night if that be not possible, prior to the commencement of the ceremony itself. As there is only the mental purity to be attempted at after these are disposed of, we may safely presume that this *Pavithram* is intended for the purpose.

Now we may try to understand if there is any explanation for wearing this *Pavithram* of *kusa* grass while performing religious rites and ceremonies. In all cases like this, the popular expressions and their meanings as well as the myths that are in reality allegories containing deep-hidden truths—at least many of them—may be pressed into service.

There is a saying *Kusagra Buddhi* which means keen intelligence. People somehow have connected this grass—*kusa*—with mind or intellect. So our statement that *Pavithram* of *kusa* grass has a direct application for mental purity stands supported and strengthened. Further, Lord Subrahmanya, the second born of Siva, is represented by a serpent which symbolizes wisdom. *Purānas* say that he was born in a *Saravana* or forest of *kusa* grass. This fact is highly significant and emphasizes and supports this statement.

The *Pavithram* made for people performing inauspicious rites and ceremonies, as for instance, the funeral rites for the dead, consists of only one blade of the *kusa* grass, while that made for people performing auspicious ceremonies like the marriage ceremonies consists of two blades. The ceremonies neither auspicious nor inauspicious but performed with spiritual significance as for example the *Tarpanam* (oblations of water and *Sesamum*) offered to the *Pitris* (manes) on new-moon days require the wearing of *Pavithram* of *kusa* grass made of three blades. The number of blades has also its significance. One blade signifies the mental force of one; while two blades signify the force of two—the husband and the wife. The three blades were intended to signify, perhaps, the mental force of the preceptor or some one else added to those of the husband and wife.

CREMATION OF CORPSES

It is a custom among many of the Hindus that they cremate the corpses and not bury them as it is the case with people in other parts of the world. It is said that the Parsis think that both cremation as well as burial are undesirable for the reason that use may be made of the body built day by day for a number of years, to feed the birds of prey like vultures living on carrion. In one respect the suggestion appears to be worthy of putting into practice. The best method of disposing of one's possession is, of course, that of making it useful to men as well as others of God's creation. This may safely be done, if the deceased do not happen to leave behind them kith and kindred, feeling keenly the irreparable loss of their dearly loved persons.

But almost all people do have loving friends and relatives and somehow they would feel more if the bodies of their dearly loved friends and relatives are exposed to be torn limb by limb and devoured by birds of prey than if they are cremated or buried. Here it is only a question of sentiment and strictly speaking all of the three modes of disposing of the dead give equal amount of sorrow to the surviving relatives.

Anyhow, the best way of disposing of the corpse is said to be by cremation, and the reasons for this are :—

1. It avoids rotting of the corpse which pollutes percolating water reaching wells and endangering human safety by breeding dangerous microbes.

2. Rites for the dead enjoined in the Hindu *Sāstras* or rituals for the dead require the cremation of the corpses. If corpses are not burnt, they say that the

tenants of these corpses could not reach the super-physical worlds where the rites performed for the dead could benefit them.

Even among the Hindus all do not cremate the corpses. For instance, a *Sanyāsi*, if he dies, is buried and not cremated. Children below a particular age are buried and not cremated. Certain lower caste Hindus only bury the corpses and do not burn them.

The reason for these is obvious. The souls of men who have reached a particular stage in human evolution should reach a particular super-physical world after death to make progress and the rites for the dead performed by the relatives lifts them up to those levels. *Sanyāsis* do not need the help of the living to reach such levels since by renunciation of everything worldly, they have acquired merit which could elevate them to those levels. Very young children do not need cremation if they die, because they have had no time to develop emotions and intellect sufficiently to require the assistance of the rites for the dead performed for them by the living. They simply rise to those levels as soon as they die.

As for the burial of the corpses by the lower caste Hindus and others, it need only be said that certain customs they follow are considered enough to lift them to super-physical regions suitable for them to remain and make progress.

HINDU DIETARY

THE order in which the several articles of diet are made use of by the Hindus reveals the profound knowledge manifested by the sages of old in physiology and anatomy. In fact, they seem to have been posted with fuller knowledge of the functions of the different organs of the body than modern scientists are. It is proposed to deal here with the vegetable diet only and not animal diet and that too of the higher class people of the Hindu community. The several courses may be sharply classified under (1) preparations stimulating glands like the salivary gland, etc. ; (2) stuffs yielding starch ; (3) stuffs yielding proteid ; (4) fats ; (5) salts ; and (6) preparations having properties nullifying injurious effects of food on the system.

A sweet preparation called *Pāyasam* is to be taken first. As this contains sugar instead of the starch in the rice, it serves the purpose of starting easily the flow of saliva facilitating the conversion of starch in the next course of rice into sugar and its ready absorption in the system.

The second course consists of boiled rice mixed with boiled dhol and ghee. Rice contains starch, dhol contains proteid and these are duly digested and absorbed.

The ghee added makes the course palatable and it also serves the purpose of a lubricant, facilitating the passage of food through the alimentary canal system. Several preparations going by the names, *Sāmbhār*, *Kooṭṭu*, *Mōrkoḷambu*, etc., are used to facilitate the profuse flow of saliva stimulating the salivary glands in the mouth.

The next preparation is what is called *Rasam* and there are several kinds of it going by the names, *Mysore-rasam*, *Pannīr-rasam*, *Miḷagu-rasam*, *Poricha-rasam* and so on. This is used with boiled rice and swallowed. Here too, preparations going by the names *Varuval*, *Kari*, *Kooṭṭu*, *Pachaḍi*, etc., are made use of to stimulate the glands. In all these preparations tamarind, oil, salt, spices, black gram, etc., are used to be absorbed into the blood and thus enrich it to enable it to build fine tissues. Substances like coriander seed, cummin seed, mustard seed, pepper, etc., serve different purposes in the process of digestion of the food-stuff taken into the system. Some serve the purpose of a stomachic, some like the substance asafoetida in regulating the wind in the stomach, some to regulate the functions of the liver and so on.

The next course consists in a variety of cakes left to simmer in boiling oil or ghee, some sweet and others not sweet but hot and so on. These are such as are capable of digestion in the stomach and the intestines near it. In these preparations are added spices, etc., that have carminative and stomachic properties.

The last course but one consists of fruits to aid in the digestion of the food and the last course itself is boiled rice, mixed with curd or sour milk which contains a large quantity of salts necessary for the body. One interesting fact in this connection is that about the close of the meal stanzas in praise of God are recited in a pleasant voice and tune by some among the guests. It is the firm-rooted belief of the Hindus that food taken with mind resting on pure and noble thoughts would go to build up bodies achieving noble deeds. For this purpose silence and meditation upon God during the meal time are observed by the wise; but the jolly and worldly-minded men and women swallow their food with pleasant tete-a-tete, which helps them to build bodies capable of responding to hilarious impacts.

At any rate, food should never be taken with impure and bad thoughts for the reason that such men are sure to build bodies capable of doing bad and wicked actions.

Further, food is enjoined to be eaten in company for the simple reason that the mind may be engaged in pleasant thoughts and conversation during the meal. The importance of *Samārādhana*, etc., lies in this fact only, viz., that the host helps the guests to build into their bodies tissues capable of responding to devotional impacts, if the feast is held in honour of a deity; and hilarious and jolly impacts, if it happens to be one given on marriage occasions.

So if people are bent on building bodies of a requisite temperament let them make it a point to dwell on the particular virtue required when taking their meals for a sufficient period of time and then they may be surely crowned with success.

At the close of the meal *pan supari*, flowers and sandal paste are distributed to the guests.

FEEDING CROWS AND DOGS BEFORE EATING

In typical Hindu families the daily meals for the members are prepared by the elderly lady—the mother—assisted perhaps by her daughters. Just as in typical Christian families, no one is allowed to eat till after Grace, so in typical Hindu families no one is allowed to eat till after the prepared food is first offered to God. The chief male member of the family performs the *Pooja* in which the food is offered to God. In some houses where *Pooja* for the deity is not performed, the food prepared is offered to the deity kept in the house. After this mental offering, a handful of the food is taken and placed in the open courtyard of the house for the crows to feed on. Only thereafter, the inmates sit to take their meal, which, in the case of scrupulous old people, is taken only once during day and once during night throughout their life-time. But when performing *Srāddha* ceremonies, this custom is not followed. The ball of rice first offered to the manes of the dead relatives of the performers of the *Srāddha* ceremony, who are not offered the *Srāddha* preparation along with the manes for whom the *Srāddha* was specially designed and performed, and then placed in the courtyard of the house as an offering to the crows. Somehow, the Hindus have the belief that if the crows did not eat the food placed as a ball of rice offered to the manes, the relationship between them and the performer is not cordial and the incident perhaps foreboded evil! Anyhow there is the indication of the belief that the crows frequenting a particular house have some sort of relationship to the manes of the dead.

The other animal fed before taking the meals is the dog and this is done only at nights but not in day-time. The reason perhaps is that crows are not available at nights but dogs are ready at hand.

From certain anecdotes current among the masses, it appears that this unique custom had its origin from the fear that the food might have been poisoned by some one. While history tells us that in royal families one member was ready to kill another to grasp power and wealth, it is no wonder that people entertained the fear of being poisoned by their enemies in those days when there were rival clans in deadly feud, and the offering of bribes to poison and thus remove from the path undesirable people was the most common. Therefore the explanation from the dark side is that people made use of the domestic crows and dogs to test the presence of poison in the food they were to take and this is no compliment to them at all from a moral aspect of view.

Viewed from the bright side we may explain the custom as having originated from the noble view taken by the people in recognizing even the inferior animals, nay even plants as works of the Almighty fit to be regarded as younger brothers in the scale of evolution and consequently deserving our help rendered as a duty we owe them.

EATABLES NOT TO BE SOLD

It is the belief with many of the Hindus that eatables should not be sold for money and that if any one did so, he will have to remain for a time on certain levels of hell after his death. Further, the money obtained from sale of food, cakes and in fact of all eatables is considered an accumulation of sin and hence could not be conducive to the welfare and prosperity of the individual earning it. There is also the belief that prosperity attained from sale of eatables and food would be but of a very short duration, lasting not even one generation whereas the gain resulting from meritorious actions of self-sacrifice and service to the country and humanity is believed to be capable of conferring lasting good on the individual and his heirs.

In other countries, no importance is attached to such beliefs simply because the principle underlying this fine custom of the Hindus is not understood. They think that food obtained, no matter from whatever place, is welcome provided it is palatable and satisfies the hunger. This is perhaps the opinion based from a standpoint lacking in the finer emotional element. The question at issue is whether is there or is there not a difference between food given from loving hands and that given with a feeling of disdain or hate.

The great woman saint of India, Auvaiyār, has distinctly stated that starving is perhaps preferable to food obtained from unloving hands. The beauty of home life and domestic bliss and happiness lies in the simple fact that the fare though poor is homely prepared and given by loving hands, the mother in case of children and wife in the case of the husband. Can the keeper of a hotel or public inn feed the people going to him in the loving spirit in which it is given to one in his house? Most assuredly not, and consequently the food partaken of there, cannot go to build up finer emotions of love, etc., in man, generally resulting in the participation of food from loving people. If this is so the principle which condemns the sale of food will appear clear and reasonable. Food sold carries with it the magnetism of thirst for gain which is in other words a feeling of grasping and not of sacrifice and loving gift. This is bad for the giver and the given, since the Hindu ideal of real living is one of giving and not grasping, in all things, and much more so in food-stuffs. Further with an eye to gain profit, the hotel-keeper loses what feeling of love for people he has.

Food taken from unloving hands builds up in the partaker thereof the mental magnetism going to destroy the finer feeling of love. In fact, if a man, though possessing a family of children, spends some years in a hotel, he runs the danger of losing perhaps his affectionate feelings towards his loved ones. Similarly one, though he may not have the requisite affection for the members of his family at first, may, in course of time, become much attached to them by the steady force of love manifested through homely meal prepared and given him by affectionate hands. Thus a seller of food, etc., cuts off a useful source for the manifestation of love in those frequenting him and hence stands condemned.

THĀMBULA DHĀRAṆAM, I.E., CHEWING *PĀN SUPĀRI*

THOUGH looked at askance this unique custom of chewing *pān supāri* or betel leaves with chunam (slaked lime) and areca-nut is perhaps the most common and considered to be one of the essentials for health, wealth and prosperity.

No occasion is considered to be auspicious unless among other things *pān supāri* is freely distributed to the people assembled. If a Hindu pays a visit to his friends or relatives, a plate containing the essential ingredients for betel-chewing will be the first thing handed in to him or pushed towards him. Surely one should be inclined to examine and find out the reason or reasons that might have placed this custom on such a popular basis.

The betel and the other ingredients used in chewing it have carminative effects. The Indian physicians of bygone ages had discovered this and perhaps prescribed it for the overfed rich. Lacking in exercise, these wealthy people required some agreeable stuff to help them in digesting their food. To avoid creating in the minds of these the idea of several doses of medicines, chewing of betels ought to have been introduced perhaps as a luxury. Moreover, it is in human nature to make use of everything found in nature to be useful, and there were these harmless but useful articles handy. So the rich people took to this custom which slowly spread among the masses.

On festive occasions people are wittingly or unwittingly accustomed to overload their stomachs. They therefore require some artificial digestives to be taken in.

So these materials were procured to sharpen the appetite first and to aid digestion after partaking of the meal.

Another reason for the origin of this custom may also be given. These materials serve the purpose not only of all-round tonics but they are also germicides on a small scale. The whole alimentary system in animals affords excellent breeding places for microbes and worms commencing from the mouth to the anus. By eating vegetables, etc., of various kinds men may breed germs in the mouth, and worms large and small in the stomach and the intestines, both small and large. Repeated betel-chewing destroys these to some extent and by helping to keep the alimentary system clean, afford no facilities for these to grow and flourish. The mouth is one of the outlets for the gases formed in the alimentary system by the decomposing of the undigested food materials taken inside. Often these emit a bad smell. Betel-chewing not only checks the fermentation and the formation of gases, but also helps to conceal, if not to remove completely, the bad smell in the mouth formed of matter sticking to the teeth and the gums.

There is also a popular belief that Lakshmi, the goddess of wealth, abides in certain materials and betel leaf is one of them. Men and women by chewing these favourite leaves of hers are supposed to please her and receive her blessings.

Avoiding the two extremes, viz., chewing too much betel and not chewing any, it appears that the use of the *pān supāri* early in the morning checks the formation of the phlegm, cleans and clears the bowels. The use of it before meal time sharpens the appetite. Its use after meals helps digestion. If people use it with discretion moderately to help them in one or other of the above uses, though not in all, they may find it conferring on them health which is both wealth and prosperity in one.

POLLUTION

It is perhaps true that nowhere in the world is the custom of observing pollution, both near and distant, so common as in Southern India. When a child is born, pollution is said to attach itself to the parents, if it be a female child and to the whole of the *Dayādis* if it be a male child. For ten days they are untouchables! Even the vessels touched by them should be washed with pure water if others want to touch them or use them!! The newly confined mother remains under pollution for a few months and she should not touch anything during the period!!! Menses woman should observe distant pollution. She should remain at a distance from others for three days. Then she should bathe in the river or village tank, should taste some salt and rice before seeing her husband and the young baby if she had one. Even babies of others should not be seen by a woman as soon as she bathes after the observance of the distant pollution unless she has tasted the rice and salt. The reason for the observance of this custom is said to be that if the woman, who bathes after her menses pollution of three days, sees a child before tasting rice and salt and becomes *enceinte*, then the child she saw after she bathed would grow weaker and weaker with the development of the child in her womb and would die before she delivers of her child. It is also believed that harm would come to the husband too if she sees him as soon as she bathes, without tasting the rice and salt. They even go to the extant of saying that he would die if his wife conceives. Mothers with young babies are apprehensive of danger to their young ones and guard them carefully inside a room till the menses woman after the three days of observance of pollution, bathes and tastes the rice and salt.

If any one dies, many of his relatives are under pollution for ten days, and even after the tenth day, the pollution would not leave them, unless and until they bathe and certain ceremonies for the dead are performed. The Hindus think that sleep is a form of death and consequently as soon as one gets up from his sleep, he must bathe to shake off the pollution resulting from sleep. So one who has bathed should not be touched by others who have not bathed.

Another form of pollution is also recognized. After an eclipse all the people are supposed to be under pollution and every one, young and old, male and female, should bathe to be rid of the pollution. Those that have not bathed immediately after the eclipse should not touch those that have bathed until they have themselves bathed and become free from the pollution.

Certain sect of people are considered to be always under pollution on account of their birth. Whenever one touches any of them, pollution immediately attaches itself to him and he has to bathe to become purified of the pollution. Some people are considered to be highly polluted, for example, the *Chandāḷās*. It is not necessary that they should touch one to make him polluted. Even if they come almost near one, they pollute him and he will have to bathe and put on a new pair of sacred thread to be rid of the pollution.

INAUSPICIOUS MONTHS

It has been the belief among the Hindus from time immemorial that certain months in a year are inauspicious and consequently no venture or undertaking in those months would be successful or fruitful. In other countries the people may laugh at this belief and call it exploded superstition; but in India most of the people would not undertake to begin any auspicious venture during the months considered to be inauspicious. Even educated gentlemen beyond the influence of superstition do respect this time-worn custom and get their sons and daughters married only during the months recognized as suitable for the purpose. The commencing months of the Hindu new year are generally considered to be auspicious for any undertaking, and the commencement of the winter most inauspicious. The reason plain and simple for the belief may be popular experience of years. There is a trite Hindu saying that every *Sāstra* and custom is for securing health, comfort and convenience. Hence we may safely say that many of the Hindu customs arose from attention paid to the popular comfort.

In the commencement of the new year, the people are surrounded with plenty having garnered the new crops. Further it is the period of rest, so to say, after a year's hard toil for the agriculturists, which the ancients were, who originated and followed the custom. So the season is best fitted for the inauguration and celebration of marriages and festivities. There is corn enough to feed friends, relatives and others freely; and plenty of leisure too. So marriages were arranged and happiness enjoyed. After the uncomfortable winter atmosphere, the warmth and sunny atmosphere of *Vasanta* (spring) is delightful. Digestion is not impaired by the unhealthy atmosphere and surroundings caused by the microbes flourishing in the absence of the purifying rays of the hot sun. People might wear flowers freely and enjoy the cool sensation in the brain and their delightful fragrance without the fear of catching cold. Sandal paste, one of the luxuries the Hindus delight in, may be used in plenty without affecting the health. A large number of friends and relatives may lie down in *Pandals* erected in open court-yards and streets and sleep comfortably enjoying the cool and refreshing southern breeze called *Thennal kāttu* in Tamil. All these are not possible in the winter season when every other man was perhaps not feeling well owing to the bad weather and on invalid's diet. A marriage occasion in which a large number of people are in mufflers with bottles of smelling salt on hand would be certainly not over-pleasant. This perhaps was one of the main reasons for fixing only certain months as auspicious for performing marriages.

Certain months are considered unsuitable for tenanting new houses. The reason is that people are susceptible to cold and other bodily ailments even in places to which they are inured owing to the change in the climatic conditions brought about by the change of season from good to bad. So it goes without saying that a new place with a new atmosphere and new water would be most injudicious to maintain health under unfavourable conditions.